SUBSTANCE OF FIRE

SUBSTANCE OF FIRE

Gender and Race
in the College Classroom

Claire Millikin

Foreword by R. Joseph Rodríguez
Afterword by Richard Delgado

With contributed material by
Riley Blanks
Blake Calhoun
Rox Trujillo

2LP EXPLORATIONS IN DIVERSITY
Sean Frederick Forbes, Editor

NEW YORK
www.2leafpress.org

P.O. Box 4378
Grand Central Station
New York, New York 10163-4378
editor@2leafpress.org
www.2leafpress.org

2LEAF PRESS
is an imprint of the
Intercultural Alliance of Artists & Scholars, Inc. (IAAS),
a NY-based nonprofit 501(c)(3) organization that promotes
multicultural literature and literacy.
www.theiaas.org

Sean Frederick Forbes, Editor
2LP EXPLORATIONS IN DIVERSITY

Library of Congress Control Number: 2017963108

ISBN-13: 978-1-940939-68-1 (Paperback)

10   9   8   7   6   5   4   3   2   1
Published in the United States of America

First Edition | First Printing

2LEAF PRESS trade distribution is handled by University of Chicago Press / Chicago Distribution Center (www.press.uchicago.edu), 773.702.7000. Titles are also available for corporate, premium, and special sales. Please direct inquiries to the UCP Sales Department, 773.702.7248.

Statement from the author and contributors:
Much of the writing in this book draws from personal perception and experience. Pseudonyms have been used where appropriate and situations described appear as free of specifics as possible while still conveying the contents of memory. We have made every effort to ensure that persons described in this book other than ourselves—and other writers we discuss—are not identifiable herein.

For Karena Joanita D'Silva

CONTENTS

Riley Blanks

Rox Trujillo

Blakeley Calhoun

Claire Millikin

Richard Delgado

"Ignorance, allied with power, is the most ferocious enemy justice can have."

—James Baldwin
No Name in the Street (1972/2007)

SEAN FREDERICK
FORBES

SEAN FREDERICK FORBES is the series editor of 2LP EXPLORATIONS IN DIVERSITY. He is the co-editor of *The Beiging of America* (2017), *What Does It Mean To Be White In America?* (2016), and is the director of the creative writing program at the University of Connecticut.

SERIES EDITOR'S NOTE

I'M WRITING THIS AT THE END of another spring semester in which many of my students are graduating from college. Earlier this morning, I attended an Honors Program medals ceremony since I was the thesis advisor to three graduating seniors. I couldn't be prouder of these three students along with all of my students this past academic year. At the end of each spring semester, I engage in a mental and professional spring cleaning of sorts, in which I become introspective and contemplative. I begin to assess the syllabi, lesson plans, writing prompts, project assignments, midterms and final exams that I have administered and question how effective I think I was in the classroom. I think about the lessons that my students have taught me over the years such as humility, kindness, patience, and understanding. I think about what I learned from my past teaching mistakes and how I can improve in the years to follow.

> "In your hands is a much needed anthology that complements and strengthens the core goals of the 2LP Explorations in Diversity series of fostering dialogue that goes with and against the grain."

My thoughts trail off, and I begin to remember what it felt like when I graduated from college, when the fears and anxieties began to consume me that summer of 2003 as I prepared to attend graduate school. I knew that I was going to be the instructor of record for a first-year writing class which was daunting. I would wake up well before sunrise to drink cup after cup of coffee and repeat the same questions: Was I ready to teach an entire class of twenty students by myself? Would I be a good instructor? How would my students perceive me in the classroom? In truth, the idea of teaching a class terrified me, it still does, and despite having fifteen years of teaching experience at the college-level on my curriculum vitae, I still get nervous every time I develop a new syllabus, assign reading material and writing prompts, when I deliver a lecture or facilitate class discussion or workshop, but most especially every time I walk into any college classroom.

I am the director of a creative writing program and primarily teach poetry and introductory level creative writing courses. On the first day of classes, I ask each student to introduce themselves, to tell me the last book they read, their favorite author, and why they chose to take a creative writing class. When the students have introduced themselves, I introduce myself as well, and then I ask them if they have any questions within reason they would like to ask me. Once, I was asked if I had read any of the *Harry Potter* books, which I haven't, stating that I was already in college when the first book in the series was published. I was mildly interested in *Harry Potter* because I knew how monumental it was to readership culture in the United States and abroad, but I was already in my late teens back then and there were other books that interested me more. A student in the class smiled and said, "Are you qualified to teach this course?" It was definitely a joke. The other students had laughed. I had laughed. It was a jovial question meant to soothe the first day jitters, but I remember the feeling of doubt and quasi shame that overcame me. I quickly regained my composure and in the fifteen weeks that followed, I increasingly over-prepared, over-performed, was overly available for office hours and could be reached via e-mail any time of day or night, and I over-spoke to the point of always repeating at least three times any commentary I had provided during the workshops of students' creative pieces. Outside of the classroom, I over-committed myself to independent studies with students, to being an Honors thesis advisor, to being asked to offer my "unique perspective" while serving on academic committees and other university service work, to giving one too many poetry readings, to being a series editor for the 2LP Explorations in Diversity Series, to a part-time job to make ends meet, and all because I wanted to prove that I was indeed qualified to be a professor in the classroom.

As a queer person of color in academia, I cannot list the number of times I have felt isolation and loneliness along with the elevated levels of stress that come with the need to succeed in my profession. I could have quit teaching at the college level a long time ago, but the truth of the matter is that I love my career and I enjoy being a member of the academic community. I could complain about being burnt out, over-worked, and under-appreciated, but at the end of the day my own substance of fire is rooted in the imagination of a classroom full of students.

I remember my week-long orientation a mere week before classes began in the fall semester of 2003, and I wondered how I would be perceived by my students. I was raised in Queens, New York City and had to immediately deal with the culture shock of being in a rural and predominantly white setting for the first time in my life. In my cohort that year, I was one of two graduate students of color. I remember being hyperaware of the fact that I had always been a student and aside from giving presentations in my undergraduate classes and presenting a few papers at colloquia, I was far from prepared to deal with the politics associated with being a queer graduate instructor of color. In fact, I didn't even know how to pose questions during the orientation about being a queer person of color to my orientation facilitators. We had discussed teaching pedagogy, how to create a syllabus, how to develop writing prompts, how to offer constructive feedback, and the importance of listening carefully in order to facilitate class discussion, but what was lacking most, at least for me, was a careful discussion/examination of the dynamics of the college classroom. There was a panel discussion from seasoned graduate students in the program about the importance of presenting a diverse and open-minded environment in the classroom. The articles and texts we read for our graduate class felt over-determined by both the author and the editor at times, and this is not to say that the literature wasn't helpful because indeed it was, but the narratives presented were perhaps too scholarly and didn't provide the reader with a sense of those interpersonal moments between professors and students in and outside the classroom. The narratives presented came across as too formulaic and clinical and didn't encompass the complexities associated with the college classroom.

As Claire Millikin and I discussed how the sections in the *Substance of Fire: Race and Gender in the College Classroom* would be ordered, I began to wonder how having a book like this one would have helped me navigate my first years as a graduate teaching assistant. This book is not intended to be a problem-solving guide, but rather to add to the discussion about the problematic contact points in the college classroom when it comes to race, gender, and sexuality. It's a text that displays poignantly Millikin's commitment to the teaching profession and, of course, her generosity and good will towards others. It's a text that offers multiple perspectives in different mediums from Millikin's former students such as the photography of Riley Blanks and Rox Trujillo, accompanied by artistic statements, and a personal narrative by Blakely Calhoun. Millikin herself has a critical introduction, a reflection essay on the photography of Blanks and Trujillo, and poems that she wrote especially for the book. There is a Foreword by R. Joseph Rodríguez and an Afterword by Richard Delgado, both exemplary educators who shed light not only on the importance of *Substance of Fire,* but also on other pertinent aspects of higher education.

In your hands is a much needed anthology that complements and strengthens the core goals of the 2LP Explorations in Diversity series of fostering dialogue that goes with and against the grain. The first anthology in the series, *What Does It Mean to Be White in America? Breaking the White Code of Silence: Personal Narratives by White Americans,* co-edited by Gabrielle David and I, features eighty-two contributors who respond honestly and openly to the title's question. The second anthology *The Beiging of America: Personal Narratives About Being Mixed Race in the 21st Century,* co-edited by Cathy J. Schlund-Vials, Tara Betts, and I, features thirty-nine contributors whose personal narratives articulate the complexities of bi-racial and mixed race life. *Black Lives Have Always Mattered: A Collection of Essays, Poems and Personal Narratives* edited by Abiodun Oyewole features seventy-nine contributors who have contemplated and written arduously and eloquently about the meaning of black lives and how they have always mattered.

For one to be an educator, one has to understand and accept that it is a noble profession. One will spend countless hours preparing lesson plans, grading and responding to exams, papers, and projects, reading and responding to various e-mails from students, colleagues and administrators, holding scheduled and by appointment office hours, advising students about their undergraduate careers, writing various letters of recommendation for fellowships, scholarships, internships, jobs, and graduate school, serving on university committees, all while finding the time to complete our own research and writing goals, not to mention enjoying life with family and friends. To some, the teaching profession might appear to be a solitary and thankless one, but I am always reminded at the end of the spring semester of the immense rewards that come with being an educator.■

Thompson, Connecticut
April 28, 2018

R. JOSEPH
RODRÍGUEZ

R. JOSEPH RODRÍGUEZ is a literacy educator and researcher in the Texas Hill Country and San Joaquín Valley of California, and the author of several books and journal articles. Joseph is assistant professor in the Kremen School of Education and Human Development at California State University, Fresno, and serves as co-editor of *English Journal* from 2018-2023.

"[T]hese innocent and well-meaning people, your countrymen, have caused you to be born under conditions not very far removed from those described for us by Charles Dickens in the London of more than a hundred years ago."

—James Baldwin, *The Fire Next Time*
(New York, NY: Vintage Contemporaries, [1963] 1993) 6.

FOREWORD: 'GUIDES FOR THOSE WHO FOLLOW'

UNIVERSITY AVENUE—a privileged space far from my neighborhood street and home—was less than a mile away from the high school I attended my senior year during the 1992–1993 academic year. Just to reach University Avenue, we students needed to cross a roaring interstate named the Gulf Freeway to pursue higher education in Houston, Texas. Our imaginations were on fire to complete our high schooling and pursue higher education in a university of our choice. So dangerous a crossing awaited college-bound adolescents that we hardly considered leaving our school and home addresses. Courage was required for the crossing as well as convincing, valid documents. For the college admissions committees, the following was required: financial wherewithal, rigorous coursework, and superior test scores. Considering the conditions of our schooling and our changing circumstances, a sole mile to reach University Avenue seemed like a great feat.

> **"The substance of fire burns, rises, and roars in these pages."**

In our schooling, we faced labels and naming that included at-risk students, culture of poverty, dropouts, gang bangers, limited English proficient kids, regular students, single-parent households, teenage parents, and underprivileged students, among others. Competing ideas about our abilities via labels determined our future. Like my peers, I just wanted to be respected and called by my name without the labels and variables. Although we were in the same high school, tracking profiled us into specific courses that ranged from college preparation and honors to developmental, remedial, and career and technical education. We wanted to learn and even attempted to learn "under conditions" that Baldwin noted as full of inequality and inequity much like those rightly challenged by the members and allies of the Black Lives Matter movement. The labels my peers and I experienced would follow us, and to an extent push us toward defining choices, predestining, to some degree, our realities: our financial aid packages with grants and scholarships, and our university courses of study, from our general education to courses in our major. These trajectories were not always fulfilling. Also, in these paths we faced professors, and fellow students, who were not always welcoming of us.

However, the phrase "first-generation students" seemed inviting and even humane to consider for us and our families. The phrase offered possibility to access and resources—and even a legacy of learning that could begin with each of us. In short, Stephen F. Austin High School was nestled near a busy freeway interchange of our large metropolitan city. Our college-bound dreams, daily longing, and university pursuits rode on many variables as we found ourselves far from the center, but more maligned to the margin or, even worse, near erasure. As senior year progressed, shifts happened like this: the variables shifted and graduation came running toward us like a roaring fire with missing fire hydrants on our school block. So much raced toward us that called for new ways of thinking and coping with resilience in preparation for our post-high school lives, especially for those of us who would make the shift and ride to University Avenue. Yes, University Avenue was a foreign space, which many of us yearned for and believed it could translate to improved life chances and opportunities.

Fifteen years later, the book *Substance of Fire: Gender and Race in the College Classroom* by Claire Millikin lands on my lap. And here I am assembling a Foreword to do justice to the work she and her colleagues collected to articulate their experiences with gender and race in becoming learned with understanding! This book holds many insights about the concepts of bias, capitalism, class, culture, economics, environment, equality, equity, ethnicity, gender, race, power, and sexuality. In a collegial and sisterly manner, Millikin includes the voices and art of students Blakely Calhoun, Riley Blanks, and Rox Trujillo as examples of endurance, creativity, and resistance in higher education. Moreover, Millikin walks us through classrooms with lenses and spectacles to the worlds often riddled by bias, bigotry, misconceptions, misogyny, and prejudice, forces that yet remained unspoken in many institutions until this volume appears and names each of these embedded in becoming learned and educated. Millikin becomes our guide. For instance, in the poem "Rain Delays," Millikin awakens our conscience and ask us for reflection and action for change:

> The measure of stars is not distance but light,
> and within light, fire's scintillance —
>
> we keep asking what is the address,
> where the flare should settle, fugitive

mirror, who will be
the one you save? (p. 128).

Under the cloak of a "surface egalitarian model" as Millikin noted, race and gender appear and "can have an immense impact on whether a student graduates with a degree that will enable her to achieve financial stability" (p. 18). Indeed, access to higher learning can be life-changing and also altering in our lives—from one generation to the next. Each of us is a witness of how circumstances, identifiers, situations, and variables can determine the altitude and levels of success we reach. Attitude alone cannot move mountains; however, joined by other forces including allies, mentorship, and support, our journey can be fulfilling for ourselves and others. Millikin notes that we who earn degrees and enter professions can "operate to uphold rather than question and subvert the power structure" in our careers (p. 15).

Years ago, while visiting the downtown Houston Public Library, I read a poem titled "University Avenue" (1986) by Pat Mora. The poem held my attention for the bravery and stern honesty the students possessed in pursuing higher learning for themselves and others. I copied the poem and then placed it on every wall of the dormitories and apartments I lived in as a student pursuing higher education. The poem eased my aloneness and solitude. An excerpt from Mora's poem reveals:

We move cautiously
unfamiliar with the sounds,
guides for those who follow.
Our people prepared us
with gifts from the land
fire, herbs, and song. (p. 19)

And who would "our people" be that the speaker mentions in Mora's poem? It is no coincidence that our people are found in this volume collected by Millikin, including the photographs of *"all people"* by Riley Blanks in her photograph series named *Stare*. Mora writes that we must:

move cautiously
unfamiliar with the sounds (p. 19)

Perhaps this is due in large part to the need for safer spaces and for dialogue and dissent to disagree humanely. For some of our colleagues, classroom teaching may be perceived as a neutral act in face-to-face and online spaces, but that is hardly the case. Instead, classroom teaching is a political act that requires engagement with students to communicate evidence, facts, and narratives that challenge the status quo and acts of injustice directly connected to gender, ethnicity, and race. Blakely Calhoun's narrative reminds us that students who possess power literacies can challenge systems as well as honor themselves to not be manipulated into performative, entertaining roles for their fellow peers. She explains, "Universities are homes and families." Calhoun's perspective is welcoming in building a stronger citizenry in a democracy that values all Americans with access, equality, and equity.

Although I made the crossing to University Avenue and gained the access and credentials to pursue several professional careers, to influence and learn from the lives of young people and my teaching colleagues, my journey requires me to remember those before me who fought and struggled for us to gain access and greater levels of equality, equity, and fairness. I see so much wonder and promise in the students I meet in my classes today. Theirs is a first-generation journey filled with challenges, loneliness, opportunities, and strife that come from family, home, institutions, coursework, debt, and employment. So much competes with one's identity and self that it can be alienating and even debilitating. Resilience keeps us going with hopefulness.

Advice from those who came before can strengthen us in many ways and assuage the fears and feelings. In the poem "Retrace," which is found in this book, Millikin reminds us, "Retrace your steps, this time do not fall," and we heed the advice (p. 131). Blanks' photograph series named *Stare* illustrates the dichotomies she experienced in higher education that were governed by "ambiguity and clarity, complexity and understanding, intimacy and carefulness; comfort yet caution" (p. 27). Trujillo's photography series named *Revision* presents queer life and the journey of naming oneself in one's own terms despite the pressures of gender bias and conformity.

Even today in the journey, I witness the levels of bias and promise held for applicants and graduates like me who are bicultural, bilingual, male, of Mexican descent, and gay. The latter was of greatest challenge for me, since I had to come out to myself. Over the years, I hid my full identities until the coast became clearer for me and in my own terms as a professor. I make the effort to know and understand my students as my professors did once for me. I want my students to know my crossing to University Avenue and my own doubts and vulnerabilities in the journey. Through literary works of study that include the classics and contemporary young adult literature, I invite students to meet characters who face challenges, dilemmas, and identities in becoming human with understanding. Here are layers of seeing and also layers of who we become that make us come alive among our students and teaching colleagues.

Overall, several identities and ways of knowing can form our interpretation of the world and the treatment we experience—in and out of the higher education classroom. Essentially, we can be dismissed or even maligned based on generalizations, preconceptions, and stereotypes held by students, faculty, and administrators. The ways of knowing and seeing we face and experience are told in various voices by our colleagues, peers, and students as illustrated in Millikin's book. This is an essential book to decipher, name, and understand the emotions and journeys in gaining an education and in the effort of becoming more humane through higher learning with understanding. The lenses presented in this book are concise, jolting, and vivid for dialogue and change.

Can essays, poems, and photographs change our thinking, lives, and world and our students' journey in the pursuit of University Avenue? Millikin's book, her work, and the students' voices presented here confirm the possibilities through change after facing bias, bigotry, discrimination, hate, and slander due to one's gender, ethnicity, race, and sexuality. To illustrate, the poet Lucille Clifton (1936–2010) wrote a poem in response to what a faculty colleague said about her while she served as the Distinguished Professor of Humanities at St. Mary's College of Maryland. Clifton's story resonated with me, since I have taught at more than five universities in my career thus far. The faculty colleague was unaware that Clifton's office door was open when she expressed her bias and criticism on campus.

On November 1, 2007, during a reading at the University of Arizona Poetry Center, Clifton offered details about the faculty colleague's commentary that led to her writing a poem. She shared, "There was a woman on our faculty who was the smartest woman in the county. I know this because she told me. 'I, Lucille, am the smartest woman in the county.' Okay, it's fine with me."

Clifton added, "She's very interesting, because I keep my [office] door open [on campus] always. I wish to be welcoming to students, so my door is always open. If they come by and the door is open, they know I'm there. St. Mary's is only 6 percent minority. They come in and say things like, 'I hate everybody. Can I come in here?' I say, 'Sure, but you must leave without hating everybody, because that's very debilitating. I think I have done good work at [St. Mary's College of Maryland] and in the county, a county of tobacco farmers and water people.'"

Elaborating further, Clifton stated that she overhead her colleague say, "What is she doing here, anyway? (And I have the highest salary.) What is [Lucille] doing here, anyway? I don't understand. Why do we need her?"

Clifton then added, "This woman did not care a lot for me. And I was so hurt. I'm a Cancer. My feelings get hurt."

Clifton would read her poem "won't you celebrate with me" to remind us about defining oneself in the face of fear, indifference, prejudice, and struggle. In the poem, the spaces and worlds that can be cold and indifferent appear in the pursuit of greater good and shared justice to make a life and living.

Now, won't you notice privilege and fight injustice with Millikin, her students, Richard Delgado, and each of us as a reader of this volume? The poem that connects the book title is by Millikin and presents the stories we live and tell ourselves to survive. We read:

To walk away from a fire, turn toward it first,
recognize the story.
Sometimes a fire has to be put out. (p. 125).

The substance of fire burns, rises, and roars in these pages. It is a fact that the quest for higher learning in this country can define by assaults, bias, chaos, discrimination, exclusion, inequality, inequity, movements, privilege, rage, struggles, and violence. We can extinguish these flames to create greater good for a just society. Some flames refuse to fan out, and these we justly call passion. Millikin and all in this book are our guides and seers who we can follow for understanding and to realize we are accompanied in the journey. Read on! ∎

—R. Joseph Rodríguez, Ph.D.
California State University, Fresno
Kremen School of Education and Human Development
San Joaquín Valley, California

BIBLIOGRAPHY

Baldwin, James. *The Fire Next Time.* (New York, NY: Vintage International), [1963] 1993.

Mora, Pat. *Borders.* (Houston, TX: Arte Público Press), 1986.

"Throwback Thursday: Lucille Clifton [November 1, 2007]." University of Arizona Poetry Center Blog (2016, June 9). Accessed March 31, 2018. https://poetry.arizona.edu/blog/throwback-thursday-lucille-clifton.

INTRODUCTION:
GENDER AND RACE IN THE COLLEGE CLASSROOM

CLAIRE MILLIKIN

WHAT IS THE PURPOSE of the four-year college in the United States? Is it a cornerstone of a just society that seeks ethical laws and customs by educating its young as expertly as possible? Can it be a "ticket" to individual economic prosperity? Or is it so mired in late capitalist agendas that it's just one more thing higher income consumers (those who have the money for it) can buy? Who has the money is nearly always determined by who has social power and that very often means inherited social power. In addition to these social questions, does a university degree even need to emerge from interactions between people face-to-face or should it be accessible entirely online? Whether we retain a bricks and mortar university system or shift gradually to online education, what are the complicated interlocking roles that gender and race play in the university configuration? Will computerized instruction increase or decrease existing gender and race gaps?

Fifty years ago, a majority of four-year colleges in the United States were all male and also racially segregated. Then in the late 1960s and into the 1970s, many institutions began to accept women college students. Around this same time, intense battles raged in the Southeastern United States to desegregate universities. Hence it is only within the

> "Gender bias, racial bias, and class bias continue to play a heavy role in determining students' fates within the academy."

past fifty years (less than the average American lifespan) that the United States has generally accepted the idea that everyone—regardless of gender, ethnicity, or race—should be eligible to gain a university degree.

Of course, that does not mean that everyone has equal access to higher education nor comparable experiences once enrolled in a four-year college. Tuition for elite private colleges has soared, placing them out of reach for most Americans. Student loans—the way most of us get through college—have created an albatross society where many spend decades paying off the loans with high-interest rates that initially made college possible. Even if a prospective college applicant is able to access (through luck, talent, hard-work, or some other avenue) a four-year college education, a student who is female, gay, trans, and/or non-white may be interpreted by the academy, first and foremost, as an "Other" rather than primarily as a student in pursuit of opportunity and academic success.

This small, critical, and creative book offers a few angles of vision, a few voices from inside the four-year college experience. We want to make clear at the outset that we do not speak for everyone. We speak for ourselves, sounding our experiences, impressions, thoughts, and analyses as faculty members and students in four-year colleges in America in the second decade of the twenty-first century. And we do not speak with a uniform voice. We speak from the perspectives (variously and not in the composite) of women, men, gay and lesbian, straight, bi-racial, African American, white, Latina/o, students, professors. We speak as artists, educators, scholars, and writers.

This book does not offer a programmatic solution to the myriad problems besetting the academy. We offer perspective: inside experiences, emotions, and most of all: urgent questions. The idea of a "substance of fire" is the metaphor of this book. By this phrase, we mean the way that issues surrounding gender and race flare up at points of tension in the classroom and the overall college setting and environment. Student protests burgeoning around the country attest to the belief held by many students that we are not yet a gender equal and racially neutral society. Our book is a place for contemplation on some of these issues, fueled by a desire to move toward an academy where not only can all voices speak, but are also heard. That said, our book is personal and analytical, seeking broader understanding through the lens of specific experience.

Standpoint Theory

When, as an undergraduate, I landed at Yale and I was overwhelmingly unprepared for the place. There were so many inflections of class background that I did not understand. I was a white middle-class Southerner educated in the often sub-par public schools of the South. And, for reasons I will not go into here, I did not attend ninth grade. I did not "skip" ninth grade, something else just happened. Even so, on the eve of entering high school, I was given standardized tests and excelled at them. And so, being white and having aced all the standardized tests, on entering high school, I was placed in honors and A.P. classes with a small group of predominantly white kids (some were South Asian, a few Latino, none were black). Our high school was "tracked." I arrived at Yale because I scored so high on standardized tests, and ran fast times (I was a student athlete, middle-distance runner). I got a university work-study job to round out the picture. My study habits were close to non-existent, as I had gotten by on standardized test scores not careful study habits.

I was not groomed for Yale, and that made a difference once I arrived there. However, this lack of preparation paled in comparison to the impact that simply being female and (at that time and at that age) a person considered pretty had on my way through the academy. A fellow classmate told me his "theory" was that the prettier a girl is, the less intelligent she was because true beauty, in his estimation, depended upon a certain emptiness. This kind of thinking was not anomalous in the place and time of my college experience at Yale. In the classes I took for my major, it was assumed that the male students were smarter and I was there in a subsidiary role. This is surely due to my initial major being Mathematics and my next choice—the one I stayed with—being Philosophy. At the time, these were male dominated fields in a deeply entrenched way. As a college junior in the spring, I remember asking a professor to act as my senior thesis advisor: I began the conversation by reminding him of a paper I had written for his large lecture class the previous year, a paper that had received high marks and enthusiastic praise. He answered this request by saying, "I don't remember that paper, but I could never forget a face like yours." The senior thesis topic I pursued was the question of suicide in existential philosophy, which gives one a sense of how I felt at the time. I got through Yale in a state of numbness, or "survival mode." Survival mode is the norm for many college students, but there are different versions and causes of survival mode.

During my undergraduate years at Yale, precisely all my professors were white. "Diversity" meant that many of the professors were European—French, Italian, German. All but one were male. The one woman professor was decidedly ill-spoken of by students, who suggested she had been hired as part of a package deal with her well-regarded husband as the faculty member the university actually wanted.

Whether this was true, I cannot say, but the rumor impacted not only this professor's capacity to teach her classes (as the students were generally not on her side) but also impinged on my own inchoate sense of wanting to find a female mentor. As these echoes go, my sense of my own capacity to excel academically was tainted by the disparagement with what students generally held this isolate female faculty member to. Though I remember hearing good assessments of her—male—graduate student teaching assistant, a guy whom other students felt sure was on his way to academic stardom.

Beyond Standpoint Theory

My experience through the academy has been deeply marked by gender. That is not true for all women of my generation and certainly is not true for all women younger than I am. Yet for many women students, even now gender plays an outsized role in their experience of the academy. It is a controversial statistic, but studies suggest that as many as one fourth to one fifth of all undergraduate women are sexually assaulted while in college.[1] A small qualitative study that I conducted with a colleague (forthcoming in the journal *Feminist Studies*) found that being sexually assaulted while in college may have a profoundly deleterious effect on a student's academic progress. Hence if one out of five college women are assaulted while students, then one fifth of women students' experience college at an implicit disadvantage. And there are other related problems: less than twenty percent of computer science majors are women. Only about twenty percent of engineering students are women. But both these majors offer high rates of post-graduate employment, close to one hundred percent. [2] Of course, this is not to disparage fields that are socially coded as feminine. Only to point out that employment in these fields is, across the board, typically less lucrative and harder to secure. For example, college majors that offer relatively low chances of post-graduation full-time lucrative employment are counseling, psychology, and fine arts, majors decisively populated by women students.

But gender bias is only one piece of the puzzle. Where I teach now, many—and indeed most—of the students come from affluent families. This is because at this university (as at many tier-one public universities) there is a trend against programs that allow students whose families cannot pay for their education to attend. That means that people who do not come from affluent families are getting less support for attending college now than in earlier decades. The College Board states that the average cost for a single college student in 2016-17 is $20,090 dollars, which is out of reach for a large number of American families.[3] For middle class families, college means student loans and these loans often become millstones, yoking the graduate to hefty payments for decades.[4] For impoverished families, a four-year college degree becomes a near impossibility even with financial aid. And once a student is admitted with either financial aid or an athletic scholarship, there may be burdens placed on the student that hinders her path through college. As a former student athlete who was also work-study, I note that students who have a job or work for a sports team (since athletic competition after college is often considered a job), do not have the same experiential access—simply in terms of their time and energy—to education that students who are not working and not performing in the sports arena have. Student athletes who spend tremendous amounts of time and energy training and competing are not able to bring the same level of time and energy to their classwork; they are too tired from training, too busy with competing. Despite that impediment, many student athletes perform well in school, but it is worth questioning whether their access to *all* majors is ultimately limited by the time and work they dedicate to performing athletically. Likewise, working serious hours for money while attending college encroaches on the time available for studying, recreation, or even sleeping. It seems one should not need to say this, yet it bears stating: economic pressures continue to weigh on students not from affluent families even once they are ensconced in college.

Once in the classroom, not all students will find that they receive equal treatment or have equal access to educational options. Returning to that engineering major (which, statistically speaking, is highly likely to lead to steady and lucrative employment), only six percent of college engineering majors are African American. Only three percent of biological engineering majors are African American. Only eight percent of STEM field Bachelor's degrees are awarded to Latino/Latina students. Again, I do not cite these statistics to preference STEM fields because that preference in itself is a cultural bias and a problematic one. Rather, these statistics suggest that once students are enrolled in the four-year college system, racial bias plays a role in the earning potential they have once they graduate. I do not mean to imply that earning potential defines a human being, that assumption is a free-market economy misprision. But earning potential does, in our society, strongly influence social status. Social status and wealth in turn influence health, and longevity. Earning potential is closely aligned with cultural capital in a capitalist society. Hence the statistics tell us that even once students outside dominant social groups and gender arrive at college, their lives are not "set." Gender bias, racial bias, and class bias continue to play a heavy role in determining students' fates within the academy, even after it affects their chances of getting into college in the first place.

Recent research indicates that even after students reach a four-year college, racial and gender barriers can significantly impede the student's progress and outcome. In a recent study, Peter Arcidiacono and Cory Koedel conclude that, "Conditional on enrollment, African American students are substantially less likely to graduate from four-year public universities than white students."[5] As one cause of this discrepancy, the authors cite "racial differences in how students sort to initial majors."[6] In other words, once enrolled in the privileged space of the four-year college, students almost immediately (upon sorting into a major field of study) lose relative privilege along racial lines. The argument that every major and every path of study is ostensibly equally open to all students, while on paper factual, is in reality and experience incorrect. Students who are not white and male face multiple social barriers, from professors as well as their peers, in seeking major fields of study that do not correlate with stereotypical assumptions about the social roles of people who are not white men.

Keep in mind that even as college significantly lays the foundation for a young person's career, for the most part people enrolled in college are just that—young, inexperienced, and profoundly vulnerable to social pressures (the more subtle and invisible the more insidious, perhaps). In my first year of college, I chose to switch from studying math to studying philosophy in part because I had one woman friend who was also choosing the philosophy major. She and I attended classes together and with her, I was no longer the only woman in the classroom. She was statuesque; she drew stares. In a class we shared, I could sit beside her and actually pay attention to the lecture rather than be the object in the room to which attention was paid. It was a social decision, but that is what being eighteen-years-old is like. And being eighteen-years-old is a condition for most students entering college, including those who are African American, Latino/Latina, female, or gay.

The Customer is Always Right

Students are, rightly, the focus of four-year colleges. However in the twenty-first century, many colleges have shifted toward a hyper-capitalist frame in which students are interpreted, and often treated, as customers. As those whose tuition brings money to the institution, students are increasingly encouraged to rate, in online responses, their college experience class by class, event by event, in the same way that a person who stays a night in a hotel is encouraged, in digital capitalism, to rate the cleanliness of the room.[7] This increased emphasis on selling the college experience coexists uneasily with another marked shift in four year college education: over half of college faculty providing "educational content" for the student-consumer are non-tenured, non-tenure track, adjunct faculty. These education laborers (despite typically holding doctorates in their fields) are paid substantially less than tenure track and tenured faculty. Typically, they are paid less than a manager at a fast-food restaurant. Adjunct faculty often do not receive benefits such as health insurance and job stability and often teach on year-to-year or even semester-to-semester contracts.[8] The assumption that professors are unilaterally in a position of power with regards to college students is increasingly incorrect.

With the "student as customer and the professor as exchangeable content provider" model, the old habits of gender and race bias can assert their force without check. The adjunct professor hired semester-by-semester based solely on positive course evaluations by students may lack the institutional stability to risk emphasizing or even introducing material that might challenge student assumptions and demand critical thinking. She may also lack institutional support if students behave inappropriately toward her. A recent article in the *Chronicle of Higher Education* calls the typical treatment of adjunct professors "pernicious."[9] The view of professors as interchangeable content providers and students as customers alters a power structure in higher education that, if it has long needed a corrective, probably did not need this one.

Gender Bias
While the adjunctification of the college professor workforce haunts all genders, sexualities, ethnicities, and races, it is women and racial minorities (including of course women who are racial minorities) who are more likely to become non-tenure track faculty.[10] Even as women and racial minorities achieve greater numerical representation among university faculty in the twenty-first century, they tend to occupy positions of less prestige and power within the university.[11] This chronic demotion of women and minority faculty sends an implicit message to students, indicating the minority and/or female professor who is teaching them is less valued by the university.[12]

To their credit, some students push against this devaluation of women and minority faculty. One of my former students, a white, gay, gender-conforming man, noted that while meeting with another student and an African American woman professor he observed the other student behaving with this professor as if she were their student: the student reached out and touched the objects on her desk, picking up and handling her personal possessions casually. My student encouraged the other student not to touch the professor's belongings without her invitation. Of course this is a small matter, almost immaterial, except that precisely such gestures accrue and shape one's sense of self within the university community. Back when I was teaching for a woman's studies program as a non-tenure track faculty, a shortage of offices meant that I was temporarily asked to hold office hours in a supply closet that also contained a desk. Most of my students seemed not to notice how weird this was, but one student—an exceptionally observant young Latina woman—wept when I brought her into my supply-closet office, asking me *Why are they doing this?* A question I could not answer, given the generally sufficient resources of this university.

Subtle gender bias can also affect tenure-track faculty. The trailing spouse (or spousal hire) system that has become prominent in academia also puts in place a silent system whereby women often occupy secondary roles: Inasmuch as a larger percentage of trailing spouses—that is, the faculty member hired as part of an agreement to hire a spouse—are women. At the university in the American Southeast where I teach, a substantial percentage of female tenure-track faculty are "trailing spouses." While students are, of course, not explicitly told that their female professor was hired as the secondary part of a package deal wherein the goal of the university was to secure her husband as a professor, subtle social cues may alert students to the female faculty member's secondary status.

Role Models

Gay and lesbian professors, while more represented as university professors than in some other fields, may face pressure to perform gender normativity in the classroom or to occlude/play down their own LGBTQI identity while teaching.[13] Professorial role models for trans and non-gender conforming students remain relatively rare in the academy, often sequestered into sexuality studies programs. For LGBTQI students, an uneasy sense of being at risk within the university persists. Fear of being physically attacked in homophobic violence continues to haunt the minds of LGBTQI students, with non-gender conforming students especially vulnerable. LGBTQI students speak of a continuum of fear—the greatest fear being that they will be physically assaulted because they are gay and/or non-gender conforming.[14] Although college students' violently physically assaulting LGBTQI students is relatively rare, micro-aggressions from administration, faculty, and even other students can erode a student's sense of belonging to the university community. As a faculty member mentoring two students who were both significant student-community leaders (one of whom was a straight male and the other a lesbian woman) as the university went through a traumatic time, I noted that support for the young man was salient whereas no equivalent embrace and support of the young woman occurred. Both students were sterling people: intelligent, kind, and empathic. Could the relative lack of institutional support for the student who was gay and female possibly have reflected an unspoken, perhaps unconscious bias? Certainly there is no way to know for certain, but as a bystander close to both students, the discrepancy was notable. In this discussion, I omit to signify the students' race, insofar as I do not want to make either identifiable to readers.

Being supported, unequivocally and straightforwardly, by faculty is a tremendous advantage for an undergraduate student. If being female, gay, or a person of color means that one is less likely to be the recipient of such unequivocal support, then this inattention becomes a kind of micro-aggression. That is nothing negative is done, but also nothing positive. While of course most students, regardless of their gender and race, will not be chosen as stars to support for prestigious post-college scholarships and graduate programs, it is worth noting that a student so chosen is conferred a sense of self-confidence that may carry forward into other tasks and life goals.

Perceptions Matter

Perceived as well as internalized racism may blight the college experience of minority students, while positively identifying with ethnic/racial identity tends to improve their grade point average.[15] A minority student's support for success while in college appears to derive more from their connection with family and community of origin than from the four-year college institution. This means that to succeed, a minority student needs to have a deeply internalized sense of self-confidence and self-esteem based on their identity as Latino/a or African American. Such building up of self apparently will be unlikely to extend directly from the university, unless perhaps from programs that specifically encounter and interface with the student's minority identity in a positive way.

Hence the late twentieth-century emergence of programs like African American studies should have played a crucial role in altering the academy.[16] Similarly, the late twentieth-century emergence of women's studies programs may be presumed to support the progress of female college students.[17] And yet, graduating from a four-year college with an African American studies or a Women and Gender studies major consigns a student to the statistically lowest earning bracket of any college major.[18] Insofar as some ninety-five percent of Women and Gender studies majors are women, this curve wherein a Women and Gender studies degree confers a student the lowest chance of earning a high salary indicates that any support the major offers to students during college may be counterbalanced by the near incapacity of the degree to help the student financially after college. Needless to say, that our society financially rewards system-engineers far above workers who create and sustain battered women's shelters indicates the priorities of our society. These are not benevolent priorities; in an ethical world, those who study so as to practice justice should be rewarded. But since for the most part they are not, one notes that funneling women students through degrees that do not much help with the student's eventual economic agency is problematic.

Babysitting the 'System'

As legal scholar and critical race theorist Richard Delgado has argued, the four-year college experience often replicates (rather than challenges) social structures and power dynamics that flow with capitalist priorities.[19] It is not that students are not well-educated when they graduate from a four-year college. Usually, graduates are well-educated and have also been taught that the very social structures that uphold the status quo must now be upheld by themselves: that they will either replicate the power structures they have inherited or be cast aside by those structures.[20] Small modulations can and do occur with minority students and women graduates moving into positions of relative social power. And yet, as Delgado points out, within these positions minorities and women often operate to uphold rather than question and subvert the power structure that has welcomed them its lower echelons.[21] Of course, one finds exceptions to this pattern: exceptional scholars, lawyers, and even politicians. But as the saying goes, the exception proves the rule.

When I began teaching at the university where I now teach, a friend who works for the Bureau of Indian Affairs suggested—not unkindly—that my job was essentially that of babysitting the upper middle-class until they became old enough (usually twenty-two years old) to move into the business sector and/or inherit money and positions from their families and social worlds. I resisted that description of my job for many years. I resist it still. And yet, by and large, he was right. Over the years (a decade now), I have become less and less willing to teach material that pushes students to re-think their social world, their place in that world. It is too exhausting and it is not the job of a babysitter to challenge the children who inhabit the master's house.

This Book

Substance of Fire: Gender and Race in the College Classroom will not explicitly tell you how to solve the problems of gender and race bias in college. It is a group of essays, prose poems, and photographs. In this book, created collaboratively by Blakeley Calhoun, Riley Blanks, Rox Trujillo, R. Joseph Rodriguez, Richard Delgado, and myself (Claire Millikin), we explore the questions of gender and race in the college classroom from various personal and analytical angles. I describe a chilling classroom situation that arose when I was teaching Feminist Theory that taught me just how entrenched our racial views of who is the "center" and who the "margin" are. Blakeley writes about experiences as a "unicorn," that is an African American gay person, who was often included in college events, boards, and meetings so as to meet all diversity requirements (African American, gay, woman) at once. As Blakeley puts it, universities avoided coming to terms with true diversity by merely including a one-person diversity checklist.

Rox meditates on the experience of photographing queer and non-gender conforming women at the university in a group of images called "Re-vision." Rox describes the problems of gender as a mode of perception, often at variance with the individual's feeling of self. Rox also looks back on why there was no encouragement to pursue an engineering degree.

Riley discusses photographing her fellow college students in her senior year in a work called "Stare." For Riley, this becomes an exploration of race, gender, nationality, ethnicity, and allure as she sees the different ways that students of different races and genders present themselves in the *heterotopic* space that is the university (*heterotope*: a term from Michel Foucault, discussed below). Riley connects the act of staring with a camera to her experiences as a young bi-racial child whose mother is white of being stared at by strangers who seemed shocked that a white woman would have bi-racial or African American appearing daughters. Blakeley, Riley, and I also respond to the events of August 11 and August 12, when a neo-Nazi rally at the University of Virginia turned violent, each with our own incomplete and searching thoughts.

By this term *heterotopic*, used above, I am drawing from philosopher Michel Foucault, and here is part of what the term means: a society presenting a surface semblance of equality, covering up a deeply hierarchical structure.[22] This term eerily fits the university experience, in our country in this century. On paper, all students in a given college should enjoy equal status as students. And yet, our collective experience (as those who contribute to this book) and statistical data of various kinds show that gender and racial bias persist as often unstated hierarchical social structures within college. The heterotopic social space is one in which all who enter are as if magically made equal. But this equality is only a condition of the surface; it does not hold in the depths.[23] All students entering a university, on paper, are counted as students granted apparent access to the full offerings of their college. And yet, patterns of sexual assault, assumption of a major, and completing a degree make that clear that the ostensible egalitarian frame is bent and skewed by many points of gender and racial bias.

That is, the avowed and written text—in law and in policy—of most universities is egalitarian. But the experiences and subtext of many students' lives is inflected, often markedly so, by gender and race bias. That is what we mean by a "substance of fire": a tinder that catches fire when stressed. Most of the time, the academy functions according to a surface egalitarian model: all students are considered equally able to chart their own courses. But under the surface, we see that gender and race can have an immense impact on whether a student graduates with a degree that will enable them to achieve financial stability. The hierarchy of race and gender subtly asserts itself through implicit discriminatory practices virtually inaudible in the spoken landscape of egalitarian university policy, gender and race bias waiting under the surface, ignitable at points of stress, a substance of fire.■

—Claire Millikin,
Charlottesville, Virginia

WORKS CITED

1. Christopher P. Krebs, Christine H. Lindquist, Tara D. Warner, Bonnie S. Fisher, and Sandra L. Martin, *The Campus Sexual Assault (CSA) Study* U.S. Department of Justice December 2007.

2. Peter Dizikes, "Why Do Women Leave Engineering?" *MIT News,* June 15, 2016 http://news.mit.edu/2016/why-do-women-leave-engineering-0615, accessed May 4, 2018.

3. The College Board, *Trends in College Pricing 2017* trends.collegeboard.org

4. Anthony P. Carnavale, Michelle Melton, and Jeff Strohl, *What's it Worth: the Economic Value of College Majors,* Georgetown University Center on Education and Workforce 2011.

5. Peter Arcidiacono and Cory Koedel, *Race and College Success: Evidence from Missouri* (Cambridge, MA: National Bureau of Economic Research, 2013).

6. *Ibid.*

7. That colleges now see themselves as businesses is hardly a secret. In particular, the practice of keeping tuition so high that most students have no choice but to take out loans to cover the costs means that colleges stay afloat by selling something the customer generally cannot afford. But the value of a college degree, in terms of class status and the allure of higher lifetime earnings, encourages many to take out loans to cover the exorbitant costs. In keeping with the idea of the student as customer, the website *Rate My Professor* has emerged. It is notorious for being an online space in which women, in particular women of color, receive sexist and racist reviews. See, (2013) The College Board, *Trends in College Pricing*.

8. Karen Halverson Cross (2017) "Unionization and the Development of Policies for Non-Tenure Track Faculty: A Comparative Study of Research Universities," *Journal of Collective Bargaining in the Academy*: Vol. 9, Article 5.

9. Eva Swidler, "The Pernicious Silencing of Adjunct Faculty" *The Chronicle of Higher Education* October 30, 2017

10. Caroline Turner, Juan Gonzales, and Kathleen Wong. (2011) "Faculty Women of Color: The Critical Nexus of Race and Gender." *Journal of Diversity in Higher Education* 4 December: 199–211.

11. Susan Aud, Mary Ann Fox, and Angelina KewalRamani "Status and Trends in the Education of Racial and Ethnic Groups" United States Department of Education Report https://nces.ed.gov/pubs2010/2010015.pdf Accessed February 8, 2018

12. I refer the reader to a set of graphs indicating the paucity of women and people of color in top academic positions. Please see, Julia Lurie, "Just How Few Professors of Color Are at America's Top College? Check Out These Charts" *Mother Jones* November 23, 2015.

13. Andras Tilcsik, Michel Anteby, Carly R. Knight "Concealable Stigma and Occupational Segregation: Toward a Theory of Gay and Lesbian Occupations" *Administrative Science Quarterly Volume:* 60 issue: 3, page(s): 446-481: September 1, 2015

14. Rosalind Evans, Julie L. Nagoshi, Craig Nagoshi, Jeffrey Wheeler & Jeremiah Henderson (2017) "Voices from the stories untold: Lesbian, gay, bisexual, trans, and queer college students' experiences with campus climate," *Journal of Gay & Lesbian Social Services*, 29:4, 426-444.

15. Carlos P. Hipolito-Delgado "Internalized Racism, Perceived Racism, and Ethnic Identity: Exploring Their Relationship in Latina/o Undergraduates," *Journal of College Counseling* July 2016 Volume 19, pages 98-110

16. James A. Banks (1993). "The Canon Debate, Knowledge Construction, and Multicultural Education." *Educational Researcher* (1993 June–July).

17. Christine V. Wood (2012) "Knowledge Practices, Institutional Strategies, and External Influences in the Making of an Interdisciplinary Field: Insights from the Case of Women's and Gender Studies," *American Behavioral Scientist* October 2012 Vol. 56 Issue 10 pages 1301-1325

18. Anthony P. Carnavale, Michelle Melton, and Jeff Strohl, *What's it Worth: the Economic Value of College Majors,* Georgetown University Center on Education and Workforce 2011.

19. Richard Delgado, "Rodrigo's Equation." *Wake Forest Law Review* Vol.49, 2014.

20. David Gillborn, "Racism as Policy: A Critical Race Analysis of Education Reforms in the United States and England" *The Educational Forum* Volume 78 (2014) pages 26-41; Richard Delgado, "Rodrigo's Reconsideration: Intersectionality and the Future of Critical Race Theory," Vol. 96 *Iowa Law Review* (2011).

21. Richard Delgado, "Rodrigo's reconsideration: Intersectionality and the future of critical race theory." *Iowa Law Review*, 96, (2011)1247-1288.

22. Michel Foucault, "Des Espace Autres" *Architecture /Mouvement/ Continuité* March 1967.

23. Kevin Hetherington, *The Badlands of Modernity: Heterotopia and Social Ordering* (New York: Routlege, 1997).

LIMINALITY:
ON RILEY BLANKS' "STARE" AND ROX TRUJILLO'S "REVISION"

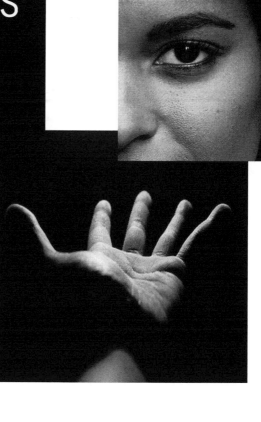

M EANING AND MESSAGE UNFOLD to plurality in the photographs of Riley Blanks' series "Stare" and Rox Trujillo's series "Revision." So much so, I hesitate to write about the works for fear of limiting viewers to one framework. But the recurrent theme of liminality—at the boundary—comes to the fore in these series of photographs and bears comment.

The photographers created these series while they were fourth-year students in college; consequently, they are photographs *of* college students taken *by* college students. And these images, which can be described as portraits with a twist (sometimes Rox makes photographs of objects into portraits), convey a haunting sense of the liminal. Every phase of life is a metamorphosis of some kind (not all of them positive), but college especially so. In our culture now, college is *the* metamorphosis: the years during which one leaves behind childhood and becomes an educated citizen with all the trappings of class bias that it entails. But the metamorphosis of these years is also real: in Rileys' and Rox's photographs of students from various backgrounds, we see this real process of becoming of different races and genders, but of similar

21

ages. Often, these photographs show us the geographic edges of the college campus and the metaphorical edges of the social self.

Searching liminally, these photographs are portraits of college students in the second decade of the twenty-first century, a century on edge when we are all on edge. "Stare" and "Revision" show us transformation, a state of becoming, of vulnerability and its promise. As the titles of their works indicate, Riley and Rox re-envision the social world through vision. Their images ask the viewer to see differently...to see anew the beauty and challenges facing this next generation.■

—December 2017

RILEY
BLANKS

RILEY BLANKS is a 2013 graduate of the University of Virginia. She is currently a free-lance photographer, based in Texas, and is the founder of the photography studio Woke Beauty.

STARE: ARTISTIC STATEMENT

FROM APRIL 22 TO APRIL 26, 2013, I presented twelve black and white medium format photographs from a series I created called "Stare." I spent a year making portraits with my Mamiya C330 producing high-resolution square images that offered an unusual amount of clarity, allowing the viewer to feel as if they were making eye contact with the subject, in real time. While I was working on "Stare," I came across many sociological elements that mirrored my experience at the University of Virginia (UVA). Elements that created a sort of dichotomy: ambiguity and clarity, complexity and understanding, intimacy and carefulness, comfort yet caution.

Despite the homogeneity and hetero-normativity that prevailed during my time in college, I was able to build a network of friends that mirrored my childhood—people of the world. Through my relationships, I created my home. I chose to photograph a representation of "my people," which means *all people*. In my thesis, you'll find various ethnic backgrounds (such as Sicilian, Greek, Venezuelan, and Kenyan),

25

class differences, career dreams, and sexual preferences. However, you don't really see these disparities in the photos. Rather by the notion of common societal discourse, you see a group of universally attractive people. I believe because of that beauty, you aren't focused on what they look like but instead the honesty of their expression, the sincerity of their vulnerability.

With the use of allure, I created likeness amongst my subjects, allowing viewers to observe what I really cared about: human interaction, vulnerability, and intimacy: the transcendent photographic experience. The men were always easier, more relaxed, open, and unaware of self. But even for the women who struggled with letting their guard down, I transcended their uneasiness with time, a glance, a wisp of the hair, and a gesture.

Part of the "point" of my series is the notion of staring at people; I myself have dealt with staring all my life. Staring because I have large curly hair, because I'm tall, curvy, athletic, outgoing, of mixed race, black…whatever the perception people have had. I think part of the reason I photographed people was to make that point: go ahead, stare at them. In a photographic series, you're allowed to stare without shame. We can gather everything we need to know from the eyes, no matter what the subject looks like. I knew that if I could just spend time with my subjects, they would let me in even if a camera was between us. I call it "photographic truth," a result of pure human interaction pointing to likeness more than total difference. What you see in the image isn't necessarily your experience of the world nor your experience of the University of Virginia. It's mine. ■

Riley Blanks "Stare" (2012-2013)
Photo Credits

1. *Debra (2013)*
   A young woman with long dark hair wearing a white blouse faces the camera.

2. *Lea & Joseph (2012)*
   A young couple (she wearing a tank top) face the camera.

3. *Jack (2012)*
   A young man stands on a balcony and wears a white T-shirt.

4. *Bergen (2013)*
   A young woman wearing yoga garments stands in front of a brightly illuminated window.

5. *Ana & Yona (2012)*
   A young couple stand next to a lake, he is smoking a cigarette.

6. *Chinelo (Che) (2012)*
   A young man lounges on a bench.

7. *Thomas (2013)*
   A young man wearing an argyle vest sits in front of art equipment.

8. *Malcolm (2012)*
   A young man sitting on steps with his arms folded faces the camera.

DURING MY TIME at University of Virginia (UVA), I encountered very few minority professors. I recall having one black professor who taught a class on race relations. I had a few female professors with whom I tried to engage in traditionally feminine topics (whatever that means). I ignored math, science, business and law. I immersed myself in the Studies of Women and Gender, Sociology, Art History, Philosophy, Religious Studies and most of all, Fine Art. I had at least one female professor from each department, a few from my extracurricular "EDLF (Educational Leadership and Foundations)" classes and another from my required French classes, equaling approximately ten female professors (that I can clearly remember). I appreciated each and every one of them. Admittedly, I was quite disappointed to find that *not one* of my mentors, academic advisors, or professors were black women. No one looked like me, and in that regard, I never really felt like I had anyone to truly look up to. Frankly, this wasn't new to me. I grew up in a space inundated with white culture and male authority figures.

ON GAZING AND IDENTITY

During my junior year and thanks to my professor, Claire Raymond, who taught a course about feminist photographers, I discovered my first real black female hero. She was elusive and mysterious, but through her photography, multimedia, and writings, I felt as if I knew her. Better yet, I felt as if I understood her. Her name is Carrie Mae Weems and I'll never forget the time I met her. It was the summer after graduation, I was interning for LOOK3, an international festival of the photograph held annually in Charlottesville, VA from 2006-2016. I had been running around in the hot Charlottesville weather, stressed about administrative duties that, as a passionate and unorganized artist, I had no business handling. I was late for a meeting yet again, and was flying down the stairs only to run right into Carrie Mae Weems. My eyes glossed over as I sighed, "Hello!" She was so kind, poised, and regal. She was the epitome of my dream woman, the kind of woman I hope to grow into some day. Ms. Weems told me she was strolling through downtown, looking for a place to eat. She beautifully described her impression of Charlottesville and how much she'd enjoyed her time there. It was a quintessential moment in my life. I could have easily blown off my meeting to take this hero to lunch, to make up for the lack of black female role models in my life. I would have had a wonderful excuse to share with my boss, but the safety of certainty kept me from considering that option. Instead, I excused myself and fled to my meeting. Ever since, I have been determined to meet Ms. Weems again. *One day.*

I'm certain that my fascination with sexuality, race, the family construct, and every kind of "-ology" was a mirror of my internal desires and conflict. I passionately studied, soaking up literature, seminars, installations, and imagery. Simultaneously, I was living the pervasive issues laced within each of these topics. My parents divorced at the beginning of my college career. At the time, dating, sex, gender roles, and preferences were a mystery to me. Racially, I was completely confused. Being interracial, I didn't understand where I fit in or even how to describe my identity. My first UVA black friends judged me by my almost perfect grammar and the Pink Floyd poster hanging on my wall. Feeling "not black enough," I ignored the Black Student Alliance, going so far as to tell them, "I'm not black." Fraternity parties were worse: I always found myself in a corner feeling like a suppressed social butterfly. With an unkempt Afro, many of my white friends didn't understand how my hair got that way. During an EDLF class in my first year, we were asked to split-up based on our race for a "stereotypes" exercise. I stood with four other mixed-race individuals (in a class of 150). Our stereotype poster was cluttered with adjectives such as "beautiful," "entitled," "good hair," and "weird." It was absolutely absurd. For a long time, I chose my friends selectively, one by one, ignoring the notion of a tribe until, on a beautiful spring day, I found myself at an international party.

I walked through the doors of Dove Cote into an apartment where I found myself amidst one of the most diverse gatherings of people I had ever seen at UVA. I heard Spanish, French, Italian, and English. I saw skin colors mirroring a Covergirls' makeup palette. It looked the way the world does, but integrated, and it felt so familiar. Having grown up in seventeen cities and six countries, my soul ached for multiculturalism. Everyday activities were dull without differing opinions, cultures, and customs. This party, this community, reflected my hope for humanity. My experiences within the international community were abundant. When this large group of people came together it was mostly under the circumstances of partying. But I met my closest friends here, a myriad of ethnicities: Sicilian, Cambodian, Kenyan, Malaysian, and Swiss. Our conversations had depth and our disagreements were rarely about the pillars that mattered to us: race, education, and sexuality to name a few. Instead, we could discuss these issues, debate them, cry about them, and ultimately grow closer over them. This made each of us stronger and more empathetic when facing individuals who had a different value system and held a different perspective on life.

I'll never forget walking down 14th Street with a group of my guy friends. As we passed an apartment complex, a group of four or five white college kids yelled down with a southern accent, "Y'all look like a bunch of fags! Except for you, Beyoncé. You come up here." It was atrocious. My friends were dressed Euro style in form fitting jeans or corduroys and button ups or cardigans, some of which were tied around their necks. I, of course, was not Beyoncé. Our eyes stung with hurt. The scene after those comments was not pretty. More obscenities were shouted and one of my friends acted out physically. We all remained together that night until the wee hours of the morning, voicing our frustrations and comforting one another.

The faculty was no better than the students. My sister, who is three years younger than me, decided to attend UVA. She was ecstatic, and I was determined to make her four years excellent. I met with a mentor and acclaimed faculty advisor. He and I had been meeting regularly to discuss my classes, my future and any advice he could provide me. This time, I'd ask him what I could do to help my sister have the best experience possible at UVA. He asked if my sister would be interested in joining a sorority. After I told him no, he proceeded to tell me that it was difficult for black kids to integrate into fraternity culture and that there weren't many "good" black sororities at UVA. He told me the only time he really saw a black kid enjoying a fraternity was in the front yard where he'd seen a young black man throwing a football. I stared at him blankly as he began stumbling over his words, not making any sense. Around this time, I started thinking about my final thesis.

I knew I wanted to photograph lovely, sensual, tangible portraits. I envisioned a diverse group of subjects and I started thinking about my interactions with others. It was once said that whatever you do often, naturally, is what you should do in your career. This was not my career, this was my thesis, but I found the suggestion to be applicable. I started to study myself and my time with others. I recognized how often I ran out of time. I had this effortless ability to dive deep with people really quickly. Together, we'd feel a sense of liberation and vulnerability. I thought about my family and the closeness I had with them despite their differences culturally, politically, philosophically, and otherwise. I thought about how much I loved them. If their beliefs didn't affect me directly, then those beliefs just didn't matter.

As I picked apart my human connections, I researched the gaze, the eyes, the melancholy, and the effect photography has on relationships. I discovered that dialogue was possible with the camera as the vessel, and the subject and viewer as the counterparts. Moreover, I found that the more time I spent with a person, the more transcendent the photograph. There was a pivotal shift in the subject's gaze and it was reflective of my very own. When I understood them, and they understood that I understood them, they could reciprocate my empathy. My gaze was validation and theirs was gratitude. Historically within the context of photography, the gaze was described as intrusive, objectifying, and aggressive. Therefore, my discovery was significant. I took a construct and flipped it on its head.

When my professors first looked at my photographs, they told me it bothered them that all of my subjects were beautiful. I was stunned. Each subject was different, most of them were in college but three of them fell completely outside of that age range. They came from all walks of life; no two individuals looked the same and they weren't permitted to wear makeup or fancy clothing. Most of them had spent two or three hours with me before having their portrait taken. We'd walked through a park, sipped on beverages, or just eaten breakfast. They weren't posed, and I barely directed them. In fact, most of the portraits were a reaction to a conversation already taking place. What offended me most about my professors' comments was that they had assumed I had only chosen beautiful people. But besides one girl, I had known every person I chose. The twelve portraits that made it into the final thesis were a collection of people I knew intimately. I picked them because they were willing to show me who they really were. And coincidentally, what I saw through my lens, within my gaze, was beauty. I had the ability to translate my stare into a photograph.

My audience saw my perspective of these photographic subjects. I knew I had succeeded when the descriptions I heard were laced with adjectives such as "alluring," "hopeful," "accessible," and "emancipated." The photographs were records of our synergy. They were not an illustration of my subjects and they were not a rendering of me. They were us. The collection of photographs proved that connectivity could exist amongst differing skin color.

Still, five years after my graduation from UVA, I faced discrimination, racial ignorance, and the many obstacles that come with being a mixed-race woman. Just last summer, white supremacists marched through the streets of the school I called home. I responded with a monologue describing my white mother's reaction to the tension permeating our society. She had asked my sister and me not to march, not to put our lives in danger. I had already decided to use words to respond to this crisis. I stared straight into the camera, calmly voicing my concern, my frustration, and my call to action. I spoke as if my black brothers and sisters were listening, as if my interracial counterparts were listening, and as if all my white friends were listening. I made it my goal to reach as many people as possible.

MULTIMEDIA NOTES

This essay also appears as a post on YouTube. Please see Riley Blanks, https://www.youtube.com/watch?v=1FZsM-9N8uWE

This was another form of gazing, empathizing, and reacting. I continue to use my platform of expression to sift through difficult occurrences. I believe it's my duty to discern what's happening around me, interpret it internally, and then respond in a comprehensive manner that reflects the privilege that comes with being raised in a multicultural family. My view of the world is unusual, and I owe that to the unconventional life I have lived. If anything, my experiences at UVA challenged me and helped me become the proud motivated woman of color that I am today. ■

— August 14, 2017

THE DAY AFTER A WHITE SUPREMACIST RALLY in Charlottesville that resulted in three deaths and numerous injuries, I wake up to an email from my mom, begging my sister and me to stay out of harm's way, to refuse the desire to march, to resist, to risk our lives. She's distraught, in a panic, fearing the worst. I immediately enter an indescribable state of numbness as my mind goes to a distant place. My mom just sent me a plea because she fears for my safety. Not because of the car I drive every day or the fact that the people I walk amongst are bearing arms. Not because of the risk of a natural catastrophe or the vulnerability of my human body. Not because I'm mortal, but because Nazis and white supremacists are trudging through the streets of our country, threatening to kill and demanding a homeland with ethnic cleansing at the top of their priority list.

A PLEA FROM MY MOTHER, WHO IS WHITE

47

> "My mixed heritage, vast cultural understanding, and elite education allow me to enter spaces many cannot. "

I call my sister and, predictably, we're aligned. We're not shocked, but disturbed. We've studied it, we've experienced it, we've listened, and we've watched. We've stood in the door of no return on Goree Island off the coast of Senegal, the center of the slave trade in Africa where people were loaded onto ships never to see their homeland again. Yet nothing could prepare us for the array of emotions we would feel when we found that our beloved school, the University of Virginia (UVA), had been rampaged by racism, hatred, and madness. Those that came before us fought for our rights and our voices so that we could continue to demand freedom in this country we call home. Collectively, my sister and I agree to use some of the first tools our parents gave us: words.

As my childhood flashes before my eyes, I remember the stares at the grocery store. "These are your children? These...black girls?" I think of my mother, who is white and of her strength and grace, and I think of the desperation I feel to give her peace. My father and his father have told me stories...so many stories about name calling, outright discrimination, and unjust regulations. I recall these stories to remind myself of my privilege.

My mixed heritage, vast cultural understanding, and elite education allow me to enter spaces many cannot. Still discomfort runs through my veins as I recall isolation at my first UVA fraternity party. I remember when a white woman tells me I'm a pretty biracial person because I have white features. A friend tells me to get over it.

"Look how far we've come."

I look at my skin color. I note how obvious it is. The lightest it ever gets is in winter when it becomes a light, creamy caramel. I dwell on the animosity and objectification it has seduced. I never thought I would live through horrific experiences, experiences that mirror this country's history, experiences that I will be obligated to tell my own children and grandchildren. Pictures of the school I love so much flash before my eyes. UVA, my place of growth, love, and learning, filled with irrational violence and bitter chants.

"You will not replace us."

Nothing has changed, only transcended. It is our duty to use our innate characteristics to stand up for justice. We know from great activists that, as humans, we are intrinsically loving. We must reminisce on our infant years, when we didn't know that black was bad until society told us so. I call on my fellow brothers and sisters to look closely at what is taking place. I beg you: Do not turn a blind eye. Do not revel in your privilege so much that you allow it to lead you to the ignorant bliss that so many choose. Collectively, we can build a society that makes my mom proud, one that doesn't prompt her to fear for my safety just because my skin is different from hers. May these words bring the hope, enlightenment and courage necessary to stand up for justice. ∎

—August 14, 2017

PHOTO CREDIT: "Mommy and Me" by Lance Blanks, 1994.

ROX TRUJILLO

ROX TRUJILLO is a 2014 graduate of the University of Virginia. With family roots in South America and in Europe, Rox currently lives and works in the D.C. Metropolitan area while developing an expertise in martial arts.

M

Y WORK COMES OUT OF questions about gender. Yes, from a gender constructivist point of view, gender is autonomous to the sex we are assigned at birth; as Simone de Beauvoir put it, "One is not born a woman, one becomes one."[1] I use women as an aesthetic tool in my portraits. However not all women are necessarily females, exemplifying Beauvoir's claim.

This raises questions such as: What makes objects and humans masculine or feminine? How do we navigate through a supposedly gendered world? Is athleticism masculine or is our view of it biased on a history traditionally dominated by men? Is the decorative feminine or is it just that: decoration? Can we perceive concepts autonomously to gender? Or does it subtly structure or distort our understanding? Should we be more critical? Annette Kuhn proposes a "new pair of spectacles" that provide us not with an education of *what* to think, but rather *how* to think. Mary Devereaux describes this critical lens as a "re-reading, reading against the grain, or *revision*."[2]

Consequently, my photos are meant to give viewers a space and specific examples to ask themselves: How might this object/person be gendered and why? Is it necessary that it exist this way or is there an alternative? Are these portraits inherently gendered or do we project gender onto them? My only request is that we should use a critical "pair of spectacles" to revise how we see the world. Rather than take our assumptions about the world for granted, I urge viewers to critically assess their beliefs.■

WORKS CITED

1. Simone de Beauvoir, *The Second Sex,* Trans. Constance Borde (New York: Vintage, 2011).

2. Annette Kuhn, *Women's Pictures: Feminism and Cinema* (1993); Mary Devereaux *Oppressive Texts, Resisting Readers, and the Gendered Spectator* (1990).

Rox Trujillo "Revision" 2014
Photo Credits

1. *Naomi*

   A young person wearing a jacket, a tie, and blue-jeans stands beside a garden labyrinth. *Location:* Thomas Jefferson Memorial Church-Unitarian Universalist.

2. *gym bag*

   A gym bag leaning against a wall beneath a pipe: the wall and the pipe are painted white. *Location:* Memorial Gym.

3. *Mariana*

   A young person wearing a very sparkly sleeveless shirt, with heavy eye make-up and black hair that has a prominent white streak. *Location:* outdoor square between Newcomb Hall and the UVA Bookstore.

4. *Meredith*

   A young person with short blond hair crouches on a plyometric power box in a gym. *Location:* Memorial Gym.

5. *fountain*

   A public water fountain next to a red outdoor track, with a distinct geometric shadow. *Location:* Lannigan Field.

6. *motorbike*

   A motorcycle next to a tall dirty mound of plowed snow. *Location:* Barracks Road Shopping Center parking lot.

7. *Gillian*

   A shoulder and head shot of a young person whose face is turned from us, the person has very short, close-cropped dark hair & is wearing a jean jacket.

8. *athlete TV*

   A photo-still of a UVA female track athlete displayed on a large digital billboard. *Location:* Lannigan Field.

9. *Kenyatta*

   A young person with short cropped dark hair stands with their back to us, on a path surrounded by snow. *Location:* Off-grounds housing, near UVA main grounds.

F OUR YEARS LATER—four years after graduating from college—I return to the artist statement I originally wrote for the photographic series "Revision."

I've been thinking about how this work came about and how I have changed, and had to change, since I created the images. The series was catalyzed by my own questioning of gender, as such, and personal gender identity due to being "mis-gendered" or gendered as male ("sir") while having short hair. Being a biological female and having people suddenly see me as male because I cut my hair short set in motion complex feelings surrounding my identity, reaching deep into early memories of childhood, especially as I was encouraged by my parents (who are both from traditional cultures) to wear dresses and long hair—to be a lady.

REFLECTIONS ON "REVISION" FOUR YEARS LATER

"White women make up the majority of fine arts students, while white men, who are in the minority, become paid artists and teach."

So "Revision"—the photographs I made my last year at University of Virginia (UVA)—became my way of asking how gender acts as a lens through which we all see the world. How do we gender or add a layer/dress of gender to objects, merchandise, attire, body language and hairstyles? In other words, I started to see how gender is applied to much more than just people. It shapes our world of objects, subjects, social, commercial, and even spiritual. Even as my original "Revision" artist statement still rings true, I think most of the photos are a superficial look at my inquiry and fulfill certain assumptions on gender rather than question it.

Two images come to mind. Specifically, the image of one of my classmates standing outside in the snowed street facing away from the camera, and the photograph of my classmate squatting on the podium in the gym. These photographs seem to me now replications of the portrait of the punching bag for this series. They all contain a sole subject in the center of the photo frame, all motionless, yet they all connote strength, strong pose, and a strong environment.

Along those lines, I now feel that my photographs focused too much on superficial ideas of athleticism. It seems as if I accepted the idea that an athletic muscular woman was "masculine" when really I should have questioned that whole frame of thinking. I now feel that the strongest photos, in terms of not being obvious and asking questions rather than assuming perspectives, are the photos titled "athlete TV" and "fountain." They make the viewer step back and really think about what it means to assign gender to the world of objects. Because by the time the athlete was projected up on that television next to the track where the university track team practices, she had been turned into a visual object. I think my photograph shows that haunting transformation.

My favorite photo from this body of work today is "fountain." For me, this image evokes so much emotion. This doesn't happen when you first look at it, but as you observe it, you notice how rigid and geometric it is. Not everyone might feel this way, but I feel like fountains have a weighted history. Whether you connect it to racism and the history of segregated fountains in the civil rights era, to gym class where different genders had separate locker rooms (its own form of segregating people), or gymnasiums that generally retain that division. I love this photo. It's not just a fountain; it's a communal fountain by a track. When taken in context to its location, it takes on a different life than, for example, photographing a fountain inside a building. The track, that curve where the races begin, echoes the curve of the fountain. Regardless of race and gender, everyone can drink from that fountain, but it retains the trace cultural memory of the Jim Crow era where, in Virginia, African Americans could not drink from fountains designated "white."

In a way, I feel that bathroom gender segregation impacts people who are between genders or non-gender conforming in the same way fountain segregation affected African Americans. I hope in the future we have facilities to accommodate people who might not fit one sex or the other. With locker rooms, it's the same: they're hard for non-gender conforming people. Maybe we could rename locker rooms to sex assignments rather than gender, like "female's" bathroom rather than "women's" locker room. Even the sign that stands for "women's" is a problem, implying that a woman is someone who is feminine and wears a dress. As for bathrooms, that's pretty easy: Just put a big "WC" or "toilet" on it and let's be done with this issue, please.

69

Considering my maturity at the time that I made the photographs in "Re-vision," I'm pretty pleased with the images. But now that I have more life experience and time to navigate and further investigate gender, my own assumptions and opinions have changed. As someone who constantly thinks about gender, I've also noticed that talking to people who don't think about gender all the time is very informative, enlightening, and necessary. I don't know what it feels like to *not* think about gender, constantly questioning my gender and the way the world is gendered.

I recently had a conversation with a cisgender female and she was discussing her views on training partners in Brazilian *jiu jitsu.* She said she didn't think of her partners and opponents as male or female, she didn't care. She only thought about their body type: long or short, big or small, light or heavy. Their body type, strength, and ability dictated how she would adapt her game to overcome her competitor's moves rather than thinking, *Oh, I'm going against a guy or a girl.* Or, *I'm a girl going up against a big guy.* I really appreciated this insight especially since I would often excuse my losses against a male to the fact that they were men or that they were stronger.

Her perspective made me realize that it is important to talk to people who are cisgender, to people who don't obsess over the same things as I do. This is not quite the same as saying, "talk to people who disagree with you to learn a different perspective," but rather more like saying, "talk to people who don't think like you." Even so, while I was in college, it was kind of like living in a society of dominant whiteness and straightness. So maybe I mean it's useful to talk to other people when they are also able to listen to you.

Reminiscing Virginia

At UVA, I saw very few people of color in my Philosophy and Fine Arts major classes. Almost no African Americans in my classes, but I would argue that Latinos had even less visibility. I had no professors of color. None. In my fifth year and after I graduated, I audited Professor Kevin Jerome Everson's class in cinematography.[1] Some students of color. In my art classes, it was pretty much all white women students. I know now that that's common—white women make up the majority of fine arts students, while white men, who are in the minority, become paid artists and teach.

When I attended UVA from 2010-2014, the queer population was not very visible, yet quite diverse and (in hindsight) widespread, but they were silent, unspoken, and only known within closed circles. Many people were closeted. Even people who weren't strictly closeted and were out privately did not "proclaim" their queerness. What might have been the reasons for this subdued presence of queer life at UVA? While for some it was a personal preference, queer people wanted to feel comfortable and physically safe in public, but they also wanted to feel socially safe, because they were worried about their reputations within the university community. I found out very late during my time at UVA that one of the Deans was openly gay. I'm disappointed I did not know this sooner as this knowledge would have created a more welcoming and positive attitude towards the gay community in general and specifically for young, incoming, questioning students (such as myself). Anyway, I did not know of any other gay/gender-queer professors or staff mem-

---

1. Professor Everson is a well-known artist and filmmaker. He is also African American. See, https://whitney.org/Exhibitions/KevinJeromeEverson. Accessed May 1, 2018.

bers (rumors of some, but nothing concrete). I knew only two openly transgender students at UVA.

Despite this closeted atmosphere, some students simply could *not* hide whatever queerness or queer quality they inherently exuded even if they had wanted to. Examples include more masculine or tomboy women and flamboyant or effeminate men. I was an example of one of those students. I met many people, friends and not, who overtly assumed I was gay. It was as if I had it written on my forehead and they had to be sure to read it aloud for everyone to hear.

Athletes were a subgroup of queers. There were more openly female gay athletes than male gay athletes (since that was probably more stigmatized among men). Even so, "straightness, normalness, and I-got-myself-together-ness" was a very common mask that university people used. An open secret: even if, on paper and in the media, the UVA administration, students, and professors are accepting of LGBTQI individuals, in real life it was more on a case by case basis and definitely *not* the general vibe at UVA. Personally, I only felt safe if I either knew a professor's values or if they had a rainbow triangle "safe space" sticker on their office door. Sad, but true.

So yes, UVA has a heavy sense of being majority Caucasian and very straight. And then along socioeconomic lines, there was a visible *power class* of the rich, like the rich international students, the rich Greek sorority sisters, and frat brothers. Students with fancy cars. I didn't have a car. I used a bike and public transportation.

But what made it worse for me was seeing the clear racial divide between UVA staff (grounds and food-workers), and students. Laborers at UVA are almost exclusively black and immigrants (and among those immigrants, also refugees). It was difficult not to feel guilty and even sick about being the privileged young kid who owns this town (I was uncomfortably part of the general entitlement of UVA students) when the workers who feed and keep the University up and running are not even paid a living wage.

It seemed students of color were more heavily represented in athletics. Basketball, track, and football had more African Americans, while soccer, lacrosse, and field hockey had more Caucasians. So sports became kind of a form of unintentional segregation. Along these lines of UVA's *de facto* segregation, everyone knew there were certain frats that were overtly racist and didn't allow black people into their parties.

Rape Culture

Along with the frats, came a rape-victim-blaming culture. Mostly that was a problem for cisgender women: it was an open secret that it's considered women students' responsibility to *not get raped*. Frats in particular were dangerous zones and it was important to be vigilant, use the buddy system, watch your drinks, and not get seriously drunk at a frat party. I'm aware this is not unique to UVA, but a problem at colleges nationwide. Still worth noting is how this rape-victim-blaming culture actually pertains to gender in the classroom: there were stories of young women who would have to sit in class with their assailants and these women students usually did not have great resources or support afterwards to handle the situation.

That brings me to one of the fallout aspects of the rape-victim-blaming culture. During 2014-2015, the infamous *Rolling Stone* rape article was published about a UVA student who was allegedly gang raped by a group of frat boys. This sparked nation and campus-wide protests and a temporary media spotlight on UVA. A lot of rape victims and sexual harassment victims came out of their silence to speak out. But after the article was claimed to be false, it negated and hurt the momentum of fighting sexual violence. What was most frustrating to many people is that a student could get expelled from UVA for academic cheating, but *not* for sexually assaulting another student.

So "Gender, Race, and Sexuality in the College Classroom" should have been the title of this book instead of just gender and race, because it seems to me that LGBTQI still face real struggles in the college setting. And even though its relation is kind of obscure, isn't the problem of cisgender women being rape victims in college more about sexuality than about gender? Not the women's sexuality, but how college men see them.

Names

When I was in college, I struggled with gender identity, but since I was not fully committed one way or the other, everything seemed okay. But life after graduation has been incredibly difficult: I was really unprepared for the world. I began to realize that my struggles with gender identity had affected both my academic performance and college relationships. After college, I realized how closeted I was and how concerned I was with the opinions of others. No longer closeted, I still get bogged down by being concerned about the opinions of others. I'm not fully "out" yet about every aspect of myself, but I am working on it.

For me, changing my name has been a step toward coming to a place where I am myself. Transitioning from Roxana to Toni to Rox has been a journey of finding myself. Arriving at Rox resulted from the fact that it held the following important qualities: very important preservation of my history (of "Roxana," the name my parents gave me). Rox is an easy name to say, but more importantly, "Rox" is gender neutral and, as an unintentional byproduct, it is also a unique name.

Almost everyone calls me Rox now. All my teammates at Yamasaki Academy (the martial arts academy where I train many days a week), all my co-workers, and new people I introduce myself to both socially and professionally. I even recently featured my name as Rox Trujillo on my resume instead of Roxana. Might as well start off with the same name I go by. The nice thing about this whole matter is that it came along very organically. It was not forced. This was also a social experiment to show myself that strangers who have no way of knowing anything about me will believe whatever I tell them. But I never lied about who I am. Funny how these things work. I sound like a nut job; but hey, that's my story. Also receiving a name feels so passive—your parents name you, a word that identifies you until further notice. Choosing my own name in this way gives me a sense of ownership.

When I look back on my college experience, I have so many feelings of regret. I really wish I had doubled my art major with an engineering degree rather than a philosophy one. Not only for employment purposes, but because I wasn't aware of my own aptitude and interest in this field at the time. I would have been a good engineer and still consider studying this as a second bachelor's or as a master's. Why didn't I see myself as "engineering material?"

So I don't have an engineering degree, maybe because of lack of awareness or exposure to this discipline? Does that matter? The reality of my life today is that I struggle financially, I hold high school degree level jobs, and continue to question my gender identity daily. It's exhausting. I try to stay positive and reflect on what I have learned and accomplished despite my struggles.

To tell the truth, for a long time after graduating, I resented UVA and regretted my time there. The classes and professors formed a bubble that sheltered me from the realities of the outside world. But now I feel it would have been better to attend college after experiencing the harshness and difficulties of the real world, rather than prolonging the comfort of "childhood" and being taken care of. Maybe I would have chosen a path of study that enabled me to do what I really want to do as an adult instead of working minimum wage jobs, which is my life right now. But the reality is that discerning the line between my story and my history at UVA has taken patience, maturity, and time. And I'm still not sure of it. One aspect of my life that I do identify with during my time in college is when I began to really search for and struggle with my sexual orientation, and subsequently my gender identity. This internal struggle in conjunction with academic and social stresses greatly impacted my mental health. It took a lot of mindfulness to realize now how truly depressed I was in college. My awareness of mental health started in college, and thanks to that, I continue attending to my mental health to this day.

Looking (or Not Looking) Like a Woman
So how did this project of the photographs in "Revision" start? A year and a half before, I had to produce my thesis project for my Studio Art major—a thesis that requires you to make a body of work in the medium of your concentration within the studio art department. Around March 2012, I decided to participate in the St. Baldrick's charity event (St. Baldrick's is an organization that raises money for children's cancer

research). At these fundraising events (held locally nationwide), people shave off their hair and celebrate baldness. In addition, people can donate their hair if it meets certain requirements. Anyhow, I thought it was very exciting and brave of the young women (mostly fellow UVA students) who collectively and swiftly went bald in a single evening.

This inspired me and I decided to try going bald. But I had many fears. What would my parents think? What would I look like? Am I brave enough to do so? It would take forever to grow back. I mulled it over, unsure if I would be part of the next cohort of women (and men) to participate. Finally, in 2012, I made up my mind and thought, *Fuck it. Now or never.* Ultimately, I raised between two and three hundred dollars. Not bad for a last minute decision for a good cause. But in the end, this was all a cover-up. An excuse. Really, I was dying to see what I would look like bald; so very curious, the need to know triumphed over any lingering fears I may have had.

And that was that: I was bald. The process was very anticlimactic. Some women cry in the process, some people get emotional in other ways. It was on, and then it was off. No hair. And when I got my hair shaved off, I had short hair again for the first time since I was seven or eight years old. After my hair was short, strangers misgendered me as male a lot even though I wore the same unisex/tomboy/sporty type of clothing that I wore before my hair was short. Typically, many women (mostly young UVA students) would compensate for their lack of locks by wearing big earrings and spring dresses or skirts. I didn't follow this path. Not on purpose, but just because I saw no need to do so.

However, being called "sir" frustrated and angered me a lot at first. I couldn't understand it. I had tried all these years to be a girl and I still wasn't "doing it right." Why? It hurt my feelings. Like I was doing some-thing wrong. Even as a kid, I had never said—or even thought—that I was a boy, but I did *not* like girly things, and was constantly reminded that I was in fact a girl, not a boy, and therefore was not allowed to do the same things boys could do. This did not make sense to me as a child nor does it make sense to me now. But I was being raised to be "a lady," so apparently all the fun activities were reserved for boys. As an adult, I understand the angle my parents came from, their upbringing, and the general gender-binary in our society and culture that is still quite pervasive today. But I wish it hadn't been my experience. Luckily, it seems to be changing and it seems more and more children are being permitted to be themselves, regardless of gender identity. I think kids just do what they like to do and don't do what they dislike doing. It's just that when people label certain activities as feminine and masculine behavior, they start crippling a young child's unique individuality.

By cutting my hair short, I was suddenly being seen as a man. Even though all my life I had felt a real distance from femininity and fem-inine activities and clothes, I found this shift in others' perception of me upsetting. But then I stepped back and questioned it. Why did they think I was a guy? Was it because I have short hair? Is it that simple? Girls have long hair and guys have short hair? No, there's more to it. It's clothing, posture, gestures, and colors. A sum of many compo-nents. I guess I checked enough boxes at an initial superficial glance.

I've traveled and lived internationally. In the U.S. and abroad, there are men with long hair and women with short hair and they don't get mistaken for the opposite sex. What was it then? My clothes? But they were all from the women's section: Old Navy skinny jeans, a random t-shirt, a hoodie, and some form of shoes. Sounds pretty standard to me. I wasn't particularly fashionable, but I was presentable. I rarely trotted "the Grounds" in pajamas or baggy sweat pants like so many of my fellow classmates. I had been raised with a certain European etiquette that you just don't leave the house that way or wear gym clothes unless you're actually going to the gym.

Four years after UVA, I buy my clothes from both the women's and the men's section. My hair is still short. People see me how they see me. I've trained myself to be less self-conscious. Rox as a name has become a new chapter for me: it signifies an open space, a place where I am not required to be feminine or masculine. My knowledge, opinions and abilities continue to evolve. I continue to evolve. And while I realize I cannot change the past chapters of my life, I hope to take the lessons I've gained to write a better future for myself and others.■

BLAKELEY CALHOUN

BLAKELEY CALHOUN is a 2015 graduate of the University of Virginia. A member of the University of Virginia's Serpentine Society, Blakeley is currently a graduate student at Michigan State University, where she is also an Assistant Community Director.

I HARDLY REMEMBER anything about college. I struggle to list more than five of the dozens of classes I took. Forgetting what I assumed would be unforgettable times is upsetting. I am not sure why I'm missing pieces of what I know to have been the best four years of my life. It feels like waking up and trying to explain a dream from the night before: the memory is vivid at first, then fuzzy. By the time I find someone to tell, the memory is nearly gone.

REMEMBERING AND REVISITING

However, from what I can gather nearly three years removed from my time as an undergraduate, my time in college was political, hard fought, contentious, embattled, and, overall, joyful. I entered college surprisingly unassuming on how my black body, female identity, and masculine queer presentation would ruffle the feathers of Mr. Jefferson's University. As I stumbled through college, my race, gender, and

> **"By performing my black identity and gayness, people came to expect things of me that were not part of my true character."**

sexuality would become my tools. I used them to garner credibility and created a demand for my thoughts and ideas. By my third year of college I cleverly exerted some traction socially and academically.

Of all the things I have forgotten, I do remember the clarifying moment of connecting the dots of how I could have been exalted so suddenly by my peers and administrators. In hindsight, what I call my "rise to unicorn status" felt suspicious. Feeling so admired and needed was a trap. I conveniently killed three birds with one stone (or in another metaphor, I was their way of outsourcing the work of three marginalized groups into one person). While I thought I was loved, in reality I was ceremonially bled out for the benefit of anyone who held me firmly mounted on my unicorn pedestal. I don't mean to sound too hurt because admittedly, I also benefitted from this experience.

Part of me wonders what my gender/race performance would have looked like if I had more educators who were of color or openly LGBTQ. Prior to graduate school, I only had three teachers of color, each in elementary school, middle school, and college (I remember taking an African and African American studies course in college just for the experience of having a black professor, only to have a white professor walk in on the first day). Would I have had more self-worth if I didn't feel the need to put on a song and dance for the white people around me? By college, I was a seasoned entertainer in the classroom. I knew how to please a crowd of white people. At the same time, all of the voids left from being "the only" in my classrooms also became leverage. My singular status was "magical."

Although I entertained for the time it lasted, things did not remain magical. I left my unicorn identity in Charlottesville, VA and returned to an inglorious reality after I graduated. Without the benefits of being recognized as "special" and for holding so many marginalized identities so gracefully (as I still thought), I was less willing to barter the intimate details of my life; it wasn't a fair exchange anymore. My identities were not getting me as far as they once had. But even if they had, I was just done. Going forward, I will try to recount my transition from a unicorn within academia to the humble existence I enjoy today. By hopping from memory to memory, I hope to weave you through the tangled passages, both those frequently and less frequently traversed.

Memory 1

My earliest school memory of being truly scarred by the institutionalized sanctioned neglect of my black identity began in high school, although I am sure it was not the first time I experienced such neglect. Let me take a moment to explain what "institutionalized sanctioned neglect of my black identity" means to me. Right before I began elementary school, my parents moved into a white school district. They wanted to give me the best chance to succeed and they did. But they dropped me into an environment that was more neglectful than overtly hostile. I had friends while in K-12 and I did well in my classes, however I did not learn anything about myself in my pre-collegiate years. I saw my peers learn their histories, have safe places to share their understandings of what was happening in the world around us, and, most importantly, be centered in a learning environment where they saw people with lives mirroring their own. So in effect, through every classroom example, every selected reading, every research project, everything, I was on the margins. I was kind of like a newscaster: I wasn't really engaged in the action itself, but I had a pretty good view and could talk about what happened for a few news cycles. So, this was the neglect. Again, giving me more educators of non-dominant identities might have brought me into the fold of my educational experiences, but alas.

Before I begin with the memory, it is important to give some context on how I even got into this particular classroom. Ms. Jones was my teacher for the first Advanced Placement (AP) course I had taken. I had to fight to remain in that class at the beginning of the semester when my high school guidance counselor, Mrs. Smith, called me into the office during a break. She pulled out my course schedule containing honors classes and two AP classes and asked, "Are you sure you want to take all of these together? The workload can be a lot." Without thinking, I replied I was sure I wanted to take them, not fully understanding why she would doubt me. Thinking back, I'm not sure what made me so sure of myself. I was one of the only black students in my classes in a high school that was nearly 50 percent black. That is how I ended up remaining in Ms. Jones' AP course.

The day before this incident, my mom made me watch a CNN production chronicling the problems within America's public school system. I watched in awe. I knew I went to a "good school," however prior to watching the story, I did not know how "bad" schools were in other parts of the country. Armed with new information from what my household considered to be a credible source, I went to school the next day ready to discuss this in my morning class with Ms. Jones. I just knew I would change the hearts and minds of the other kids in my class, I just knew. Perhaps I was so confident because I had never seen the side of my classmates or teacher that I would see that day.

In class we ended up coming together in a circle for something unrelated to what I wanted to discuss, but of course I found a way to bring it into the conversation. Most likely out of turn, I remember confronting one of my classmates and saying, "But not all public schools are the same and, depending on what kind of high school you go to, you may not be as likely to go to college." My classmate came back with, "That's not true, if you can't go to college that means you're stupid." I'll spare you the rest of the back and forth, but as the entire class was coming for me, Ms. Jones watched and did nothing. Actually, she did do something: she was eating cauliflower and grinning at the blood sport happing before her. What hurt me most then, and still hurts now, is that she knew the truth. She knew I was right. As a public school teacher, she knew of the disparities, but she didn't say a word. Licking my wounds, I gained another level of consciousness that helped me figure out where I stood among my peers. I was welcomed to be in their space, but warned not to get too comfortable.

I started a broader discussion of race and gender in the college classroom with a story from my high school classroom because this is where race and gender first converged with my academics. Where I first started to catalogue my experiences as black, gay and female in an academic space.

Memory Interlude
I didn't realize how much I was forced to "perform" my identities until I was in college. Performing was always my fallback because I was convinced my experiences weren't the real thing. In all of my classrooms, I was reminded that I wasn't the "typical black student," and that even though I was "good, for a black girl," I still wasn't going to be in their club. I grew up thinking that the black kids who weren't in my class-

85

es had the most authentic black experiences. I performed because I believed myself to be an imposter. However, by performing my black identity and gayness, people came to expect things of me that were not part of my true character. Like any performer, I lived for a captive audience. So I kept performing, be it in my college classrooms, with my college friends, or anywhere I occupied. Performances varied from pretending to know all aspects of the black experience (I didn't and I still don't), acting as an authority on the gay black experience (I only knew what I read on the Internet, but that was more than anyone else around me knew), and, a personal favorite, pretending to be a voracious reader (I hated reading, but I wanted people to think I was a cultured, well-rounded, black lesbian).

College

In the beginning of my time at the University of Virginia, I defaulted to write about my experiences with race and gender. Whenever a professor gave me the option to write about a topic of my choice, I always chose race, gender, sexuality, or a combination of the three. I assumed those were the topics I knew the most about, topics I could write about at a college level. Although I made it to college, I was not sure if I was capable of the level of work my professors would require. This is why I relied on my identities as fodder for my papers: they were familiar stories. Also, I figured I could get away with speaking in broad strokes because my professors were (to my knowledge) white and straight. How could they tell me what I wrote was wrong, right?

Writing went well at first. Ideas and concepts flew from my fingers, every point hitting hard, or so I thought. In the back of my mind were the times I had in high school, such as those in Ms. Jones' class where my "proof" of injustices was not enough; and the times in high school where I was so confident, only to be put down. In spite of all of this, I attempted to persist. I turned in my papers with confidence; like so many first year college students, I thought my work was good enough in such an environment. I spent the next week anxiously waiting for my professor to be done grading. Something in me just knew I would be thanked, maybe even praised, for sharing something so intimate. Surprisingly to me then (but not so much now), my professor tore my paper apart.

My paper was authentic to the black, female, gay experience I had come to perform at seventeen years old, however, it wasn't academic enough. It wasn't cited. It wasn't backed up with evidence. In essence, my first college paper was an extended Facebook rant. It was emotional and while it felt to me like common sense, apparently it was not suited for the academic realms. After that I was scared to write about my blackness or any of my other identities. I thought the topic was the issue, I assumed that it wasn't very collegiate to write about being a black gay woman. So I left the topic alone. My professors told me to "shut up" or prove it with the literature dominated by scholars whose thoughts and reasoning were out of my realm of comprehension as a first year college student.

Please don't misunderstand. As a graduate student, I understand the importance of engaging with the literature to make any point. After all, a citation is all that separates academic writing from a conspiracy theory. But with this said, having my experiences with race, gender, and sexuality be equated with conspiracy theories once again in a classroom felt wrong. Then in college, I had flashbacks of not being good enough throughout my earlier schooling. As a college freshman, I was still not credible enough to tell my story. In the moment, I thought my stories were pushed back because I was somehow, once again, not "black enough." Was my performance not convincing?

That's something you learn when you're black from the suburbs—you're black, but not the kind of "black" that people come to expect. As young as eight years old, I was encouraged to consider that I was a privileged black person and as penance, I should hush about the problems I faced as a result of my race. At least I got the chance to go to a white school. I am a black gay woman, but surely, I am privileged. My identities were often neglected in classroom spaces or used as qualifications for commentary, but at least I was in those spaces. It can be hard to explain my privilege to others, especially when their basic diversity training spent two hours helping them understand that I, as their white, straight, and male opposite, was the target of their agency. My challenges were unique, but in a way, I have always felt privileged to have the struggles I have.

So, during my first year in college I had not yet learned how to use my race and gender to my advantage. Leveraging my experiences in the classroom was not working. I remember not feeling special anymore. This is not unique. Many college freshmen come to realize that they are not as smart or accomplished as they were made to feel in high school once they come to college. However, I felt this to a deeper extent. I had played what I believed to be my best card and came back with nothing. To my surprise, I recovered and came to prominence as a mythical figure in my third year of college. I was, and I mean this sincerely, a unicorn.

Unicorn
My particular mode of performing and hustling my race, gender, and sexuality in college always made me noticeable. I caught the eye of my professors and classmates. My ideas were "compelling" and "added value to the conversation" (I got these comments on almost all of my

assignments). But in my third year of college, I became a star. I was a literal unicorn: fictional, but real enough to put on a university committee. Let me back up a bit.

When I first came to college, I was not involved in any student leadership. I had joined the Queer Student Union as a member, but I was not doing anything else. It was not until the end of my second year where I realized all my peers were shooting up the social ladder. They were in several clubs, on track to be in leadership, and gaining recognition among high-level administrators. When I had this "ah-ha" moment, I still wasn't sure if leadership was for me. I wanted what came with it, but I didn't know if I could get there. I was still wounded from having my first-year papers getting shot down for not being academic. Seems like an odd thing to be hurt for so long about. But seeing no way out but up, I took a chance on student leadership. This change helped me find my voice in the classroom.

I morphed into a unicorn as I got my feet wet with student leadership. Administrators, professors, and peers noticed something different about me. I was more relatable than other black students, meaning to them I did not seem as "black" (this was a near disadvantage to telling my story in the classroom, but was an asset outside of it). You see, in the college leadership circles, no one needed much proof or a citation on my experience. As I had wrongly assumed in my first college classes, I was right to assume that my performance would go unchecked as a student leader. In addition to living a black life more pleasing to my white peers, I was black, female, and gay¬- quite the trio at a predominantly white institution in the South. Why have three students representing three communities on a five-person committee when you can just invite me to sit in? That was the peak of my unicorn-ness. I knew why I was being put on committees, given a look behind the curtain, and being invited to places I knew would never invite people like me, but I didn't mind. I felt more powerful than ever. Not just powerful, I felt more appreciative of my race, gender, and sexuality. It made me feel special in a way that was finally doing something to lift me up. I felt like I was on a pedestal, finally elevated enough to look down on my elementary and high school peers who had thought so little of me.

I cannot decide if I still feel special because of my trio of marginalized identities. I revisit the thought from time-to-time, each time contemplating it without resolution. Do I love and accept myself for who I am or am I seeking out places where I can use my identities to my advantage? Isn't it my right to finally get something good out of this positionality? Regardless, I continued to find places where my race, gender, and sexuality would multiply into more positive experiences, and in time, I found the sociology department at my university as one of those places.

Class Revisited

As a Sociology major, I got a chance to use my identities to my advantage. No longer was I studying the mechanics of college writing or hard sciences, I studied society. And if my experiences as a gay black woman were relevant anywhere, they were in my new courses. As I took more Sociology classes, I could not tell if they were easy or if I was just good at them. We were discussing how race and gender affect our basic understandings of society. I still recite a line from my social theory professor, Dr. Stephan Fuchs: "Social science is the attempt to make an objective truth out of a subjective reality."

Suddenly, I did not have to take a chance by offering my life experience, my professors asked me. My peers were interested in what I had to say. I was affirmed from all sides, my grades were great, and I loved what I studied. If it feels like I am building up these experiences of affirmation and inclusion of my race and gender in my college classrooms, you have caught on well. I had taken these classroom environments for granted. How? I am still figuring that out.

The End of an Era

After four years of college and a year off from academia, I am now a graduate student studying student affairs administration. Student affairs as a field is all about affirmation, student success, making students on the margins feel like they matter, and everything that comes with making these ideals a reality. My graduate classes mirror those I once appreciated as an undergraduate student. During the first year of my program, most of my professors were black women; I had only had two black teachers before college and only one in college. My graduate professors taught me that my knowledge and experiences were legitimate. They also taught me how to prove my experiences were not an anomaly.

However, as I progressed through my first year of graduate school, I began to get tired of sharing my experiences and with that came a new perspective. My cohorts, who are predominantly people of color, took the stance that people of color should not have to explain themselves in the classroom. Moreover, they felt (and I felt, to a degree) that we had shared enough in all the previous years of our education, K-college. Our lives had been the subject of too many class reflections. We had been placed on too many committees to help someone take a shortcut, though we were certainly qualified to be there. We had been looked at too often to respond to the public execution of another black person by the police. We were collectively grieving from being bled out for far too long on public display. In short, we were done with doing favors for the academy. Our professors understood these realizations, and I am sure many of them felt the same way.

It was not until recently that I realized how I wanted to be valued and instructed in the classroom: I went from wanting to have the space to share my experiences with race, gender, and sexuality to demanding the focus on my skin color be removed from my educational experience. So, I decided that it was time to hang up my skates. I just stopped performing my identities. I found comfort from people of color who collectively decided to stop entertaining others at their own expense. I wanted to honor myself at least that much; I have a real experience and story to tell, it does not need any embellishments. In graduate school, I felt like my experiences were being improperly used to an extent. All the suffering I had endured from grade school to high school was being fed to my white colleagues for their growth at the expense of mine. I hit my saturation point and I think that point is coming quicker for youth of color today than it did for me.

I don't know where I am now. I know that I am more cautious than ever of how I want to exist in an academic space. Too much has transpired for me to just share like I did in my undergraduate sociology classes. I am not sure where even I can find value in my experiences, let alone my peers. I am unsure if I have outgrown the moments of doubt planted in me by my high school teachers. I don't know if my doubt and insecurities are done growing or if they are still looking for more room to expand. Once you've seen a person who looks like your father, your cousin, your uncle, get murdered on video on a social media feed reposted right under a video for how to make pull-apart bread, things are just different. I wanted to use my race and gender to make me special again like it did in college, but it wasn't all that special anymore. I wouldn't go as far to say I feel used by academia, but I do feel used up. Nothing I could share within the classroom would add much to the national dialogue. These are stories we have all heard many times over, stories that no longer carry the weight they once did even a few years ago.

Today

The college classroom went from a place where I would hide within my thoughts, to a place where I found space for them to be used for me and not against me, to no longer wanting to share. In fact, I often wonder if I have forgotten what it was like to be the only black kid in a class where no one wanted to hear what I had to say. Where I had to assimilate to survive. I wonder what example I am setting for those future college students who I will encounter as a Student Affairs Professional. Is it okay to ever stop sharing? I will never stop having feelings about race, gender, and sexuality in academia. However, I don't know where I fit in the conversation anymore. These days I prefer to moderate conversations on race and gender rather than offer myself up as a topic of conversation. Perhaps my positionality has shifted where I find myself in the classroom. Graduate school is a beast of its own, and nearly everything else in my life feels more important and daunting than what occurs inside the classroom.

Yet the events on August 11 and August 12 in Charlottesville, VA, the hometown of my alma mater, reminds me that academia still has a role in facilitating national dialogues, so maybe I shouldn't give up on sharing my voice any time soon. Charlottesville is my home. I have never felt more loved, more part of a community than in the four years I spent there as an undergraduate. For all of its flaws, Charlottesville and the University of Virginia gave me everything I have in this world. All my confidence is derived from the people and opportunities I had while I was there. To see Charlottesville fall victim to an attack by white supremacists was heartbreaking. I felt embarrassed, ashamed, and hurt all at once.

Not long after feeling this rush of emotion I felt as if I had predicted August 11 and August 12. As far back as high school in Ms. Jones' class, I was trying to speak my truth. Even in college, I was trying to get my professors to understand how it felt to be a black person attending a PWI (Predominately White Institution) or how real my self-doubt was because of the teachers I had from elementary to high school, but all the while, it felt like academia was asking me to "prove it." Now all the proof in the world could not have stopped the academy from being "shocked" by what took place in Charlottesville those two days. I had begged to be heard to the point where I was tired of sharing. I had tried to use my race and gender as bait for someone, anyone in my classes to care about what my people and I were going through, but it was all "theoretical" for them.

We treated the past as something that was overcome, not something that was still taking place. Now after August 11 and August 12, maybe we all understand. The discourse around race, gender, and sexuality in the classroom should be taken more seriously now, both by those who engage in discourse and those who facilitate such conversations. The messages we perpetuate and give life to are being taken out of the classroom and used to make policy, to fight for (or against) others' humanity, and to shape the beliefs of a society desperately looking for the truth.

How I see myself as a gay black woman took form in my sociology classes. I grew in my identities as we discussed Foucault and Bourdieu. I acknowledged the role my experiences as the only black student in a high school honors course had on my psyche in class dialogues facilitated by an affirming professor. Things only changed when I left the incubator Charlottesville was for me. I was forced to hatch, and it was a tough transition. I saw how unmoved the world truly was, leading me to believe I was existing within a fantasy for four years. Taken out of the warmest educational environment I had ever been in, my desire to share my struggles as a gay black woman navigating academia waned. I struggled to find the point anymore; there was no more apparent value in my stories. Looking back, our conversations were filled with affirmations but missed important calls to action.

With all of this said, academia is also home to many students, faculty, and staff who were on the side of those who came to wage attack in Charlottesville in August. I believe we threw away an opportunity for discourse when we ostracized those members of our community. No, we should not have given greater credence to their messages of hate, but we should acknowledge their existence. Humanization should always be at the core of an academic institution.

Faculty members should approach their disciplines with the objective of humanizing the people in their texts and the students in their class. University administrators should ensure their policies are attached to the future of all their students, not just the ones who make themselves visible. I know the long-lasting impact of being pushed to the margins in your classroom: looking from the outside in breeds resentment and discourages empathy. As I have recounted in this essay, I remember the feeling of taking a course where I was a human who was there to learn, not a human who was there to be taught. I remember my professors lowering academic pretense and allowing me to be a true learner. Universities are homes and families. Helping more students integrate themselves into conversations within their classrooms, rather than accepting their performances, is a step towards helping them realize their own humanity, allowing them to extend this experience to their peers.

I am not sure what my relationship to academia will be once I graduate again this year. I once made it my mission to fight for stories like mine to be told within academic spaces. But now, knowing and having experienced the grieving taking place within communities of color and all minorities, I will never again use my experiences with race, gender, and sexuality as war stories for credibility. Academia can take or leave me, but they will no longer convince me that my only worth in a classroom is to incite sympathy through the power of my stories. I may continue to recount how I have faced racism and sexism in the classrooms of my life, but I will do so on my own terms. And for now, those terms remain unwritten. I suppose I will know when the time is right to memorialize them. This is just the beginning. ■

CLAIRE MILLIKIN

CLAIRE MILLIKIN is an award-winning poet and scholar of ten books. Her poetry books include *After Houses-Poetry for the Homeless* and *Tartessos and Other Cities;* and scholarly works such as *Witnessing Sadism in Texts of the American South.* Since 2007, she has taught at the University of Virginia.

T O PARAPHRASE Kwame Anthony Appiah, race is a story, a story we tell each other, and tell ourselves, so often and so vehemently it be-comes the world.[1] Higher education is also a story we tell ourselves: that does not mean that what we teach, and learn, in four-year colleges is false, made-up, or fabricated. Rather, it is held in place by beliefs and assumptions about who should and

PARABLES

could be enrolled and teaching in the university. These beliefs and assumptions are also stories we tell ourselves, and that telling can make them real. In this essay, I want to comment, through memory, on some small part of that story. But I am not a linear storyteller; my mind works through parables,[2] and parallels. Writing this essay, then, I am mindful that memory is a one-sided wall, and I am writing from memory. If I offer parables about myself and about my experience teaching, the heart of *Substance of Fire* appears in the words and photographs of my former students, Blakeley Calhoun, Riley Blanks, and Rox Trujillo, and in the words of colleagues R. Joseph Rodríguez, and Richard Delgado.

> "This book is called the *Substance of Fire* because of the material consequences of gender and race, the way that we can say we are all equal but inequality emerges at the level of materiality . . ."

In this twenty-first century era that some argue is post-gender and post-race, the power structures of gender and race often run underneath the carefully-controlled surfaces of the higher education classroom, always at the edge of catching fire. In fact, in this essay, I use the word "parable" to indicate the stories that serve as symbols or stories that may catch fire. The parables work as personal essay, in the older sense of the word—essay meaning, assess, try, sound. The goal is to begin with the personal so as to launch deeper critical thinking. My life isn't that interesting, and remembering isn't an end in itself, but a spur to the next level of knowledge.

The idea of feminist theory is to take in all that you know, from studying and living, of structural and social inequality, and think toward ways to change the balance.[3] It is not necessarily a way of thinking that lends itself to parable, and yet because of the tradition, in feminist thinking, of bringing the so-called private into the public, I work through these parables of my earlier self to understand what motivates me, for better and for worse, in the classroom. The classroom is also a private/public space, one that holds theory and also emotion, one that is performative, but also, sometimes, as sincere as it gets. More than anything else, the academy is a site of power struggles that are suppressed and silenced: the power struggle between humanities and "hard" sciences (the assumption that only Sciences, Technologies, Engineering, and Mathematics (STEM) field studies are "real"); the power struggles between departmental terrains (where does Sociology end and Media Studies begin; who is properly allowed to teach about race, religion, and so on); the power struggles among difference in gender, sexuality, class, and race that are all assumed equal within the academy but that in fact do not enjoy equal earnings, respect, and opportunity to shape academic policy.

Feminist Theory: 101
Another aspect of feminist theory is the argument that one should write openly from the social world one inhabits, that is, not obfuscate one's own place in the system. Hence, for the first parable, I provide a story about my infancy. I am a white woman from the Southeastern United States whose earliest memories are of the Chinese enclave in Southeast Asia where I spent my infancy. I do not mean that my earliest memories of other races are the Chinese people with whom I lived in infancy: I mean my earliest memories of human beings, as such, are of the Chinese with whom I lived in infancy. For whatever reason, maybe due to my mother's debilitating pregnancy with my younger sister, in my earliest recollections I do not remember my mother.

But I remember the family who lived in the apartment next door; they were a Chinese family living in the Southeast Asian country of Singapore. The first friend I recall was the son of this family; I was almost two, and he was almost three, when we cemented our friendship based on a shared interest in running up and down the hallway. The family welcomed and fed me when I toddled over, uninvited I would imagine. I remember also the woman who cared for me as my mother could not; she spoke only Chinese, so that was one of my early languages also.

Amah, a term signifying a young child's caretaker and which can be translated as "milk mother," fed me salty soups that were intended to heal me—during this time, I had a serious childhood illness—and she sang to me, songs that I sometimes feel I can almost call up but then cannot remember, not surprising for songs heard only as an infant. (Years later, when I was in graduate school in New York City, I would walk to Chinatown, in lower Manhattan, some Saturdays and just be there, listening for some trace of memory, language, and first song. I was at the time taking some comparative literature courses, and looking back I don't know why I never pushed out of the Indo-European language family. Maybe it felt too emotional to study Chinese. Or maybe my life was just already too hard and Indo-European was my path of least resistance, in language as in culture).

When my family returned to the United States, I was not quite three years old and though, of course, I had no concept of "race." I knew language, music, food—that is, I felt the loss of hearing Mandarin and Chinese songs and the loss of eating food Amah made for me. I was so young when we left Southeast Asia that what I remember are those elements very close to the skin, ears, eyes, and mouth: Amah's hands, her songs, what she cooked. If fragmentary, the images from this time, all before my third birthday, are also very close-up and taut, as if one saw a painting by pressing one's eyes against it. Amah and the family who lived next door formed an entire world, my world for a time.

Thus, moving to the United States just before I turned three, a feeling of loss, insuperable, marks these earliest memories. In this sense, my first experience of race was as a category constituted by loss, loss of specific people, and their language, music, and food. In Georgia (USA), where we returned to live, no one sang the songs I had heard in my earliest infancy. I do not want to mystify through nostalgia what I am writing here about Southeast Asia. It is important to note that, while the neighboring Chinese family and Bingwen, their child who was my friend, were in a similar economic bracket to my family, Amah, as we called her, was paid to take care of me. The fact that I knew her only as "Amah," nurse, nanny, or, more accurately "nourishing mother," rather than knowing her name is telling (as an adult, I asked my mother what was Amah's real name, and she had no clue).

My memories of Amah are of her words, her songs, and how, during my illness, she fought for me, finding a doctor, and then a hospital. She fed me soups intended to bring back health, and fought my mother to give me this medicine, her medicine. Why did she do this? If I knew her name, maybe I could find her now and ask.

Classroom Parable

In the late 1970s (five years after my family left Southeast Asia) back in the deep U.S. South of my family's origins, I fell in love with my second-grade teacher. I do not mean that I had an erotic relationship with her. No, I mean that she seemed to me a wonderful person in the way that young children will sometimes find an older person full of wonder, and awe. I think this kind of affection happens when young children encounter a great teacher. After a first-grade teacher who was elderly, white, and smacked our hands with her ruler when we misbehaved, my second-grade teacher was a dream: young, fresh out of teacher-college, pretty, and full of progressive and engaging lessons. More than that, she and I shared the same first name, which made me feel among the elect (at the time, the name Claire was not a common name in America).

For me, this teacher stood for the qualities of intelligence and a grace that came through learning: a way out of my situation in my family. In her classroom, I was not abused, but seen as intellectually advanced, the smartest kid, a positive identity that to some degree I carried with me afterwards. For example, during our class poetry section, in early winter, she chose one of my poems to read aloud to everyone and after reading it she said to me, "You are the most creative child I have ever known."

It meant everything to hear her praise. She said I was extraordinary, and that was not what I heard about myself at home. Later in the spring when it became visible that she was pregnant, I was so excited I hand-sewed a christening garment for her unborn child. (It had not occurred to me that she might not be Christian.) She sweetly accepted the dress, saying she would "fold it to her heart," which I think was a polite way of saying she would not be putting this awkwardly sewn garment on her child. In any case, the teacher was biracial and, as her pregnancy became more visible, some white boys in the class—eight year olds—began making jokes about not knowing what color her unborn child would be; some of the boys even joked that the child might be born part animal.

The second-grade class was about 30 percent African American. (The town had been desegregated about a decade before us, so desegregated classrooms were not brand-new, but they were not old-hat either.) The African American children stayed out of the fray, self-protectively saying nothing as the jokes about our teacher's pregnancy circulated. I did not participate in the jokes. I adored my teacher, but I did not fight the boys either as a bystander. I was afraid of those boys, yes, but also

I was eight years old and did not understand what was at stake. Their jokes were cruel, and the teacher got wind of them. She confronted us, as a class, tearfully. She spoke about race with a frankness that was new to our ears: what race meant to her as a mother-to-be, her love for her unborn child, and how hurtful it was that we taunted her and her unborn child. After that, it was clear our teacher just could not wait to get away from us. She never came back to our school.

These two parables are personal and signposts in my reflection. I do not think they necessarily have a larger meaning, outside the personal. And yet, being personal, race is also always a category that should be theorized and removed by logical analysis from the realm of sentiment and emotion, as much as possible (though of course it is not possible to ever entirely move beyond emotion); even so, the impact of beliefs about race, and actions taken on the basis of those beliefs, is often deeply personal. What I am, in fact, describing is one version of American whiteness through a sliver of time and self. Given the hardships of my childhood and adolescence that included early childhood abuse and punishment during adolescence for trying to run away from the abuse, I'm still here, writing and alive, because of white privilege: I had a second chance after unspeakable trauma. Nevertheless, I have not experienced whiteness as a stable shelter. That is, my family setting and other predominantly-white social situations in which I've found myself were not always safe and secure. This informs my understanding of race.

I am not sure if the above biographemes (Roland Barthes' word for slivers of personal information[4]) with which I began shed much light on anything else that is written in this book. The biographemes provide a background about where I came from, when I found myself teaching, as a non-tenure-track lecturer, in a prestigious, four-year university in the American Southeast. I was, by then, almost forty years old, and had spent my adulthood avoiding the Southeastern United States as much as possible. Moreover, I spent my adult life ambivalent about teaching and the academy by living a bohemian, avoidant life, living off the grid at times. To begin the story in the middle, I was, a middle-aged university lecturer, back in the Southeast, and teaching college students who were privileged, well-educated, and in most cases white.

Teaching College

Having previously had an oblique relationship to the academy, I was unprepared for the way that college students interacted with female faculty. (I had earned my doctorate while living in New York City and during that time did my work and kept my nose down, not interacting with or learning about departmental politics, earning my living outside the university system.) To be sure, most of my students at this South-eastern research university were and are great people—smart, polite, good-hearted, and inspiring. Make no mistake: some of my former students at the University where I taught changed my life, much for the better. But I was shocked to find that a small number of male students would try to flirt with me, while some women students would confess incredibly personal details during routine office hours, seeking moth-erly care.

These behaviors made it clear to me that, by such students, I was not seen as a professor but as a woman: either a woman with whom one could want to have sex or a woman who should behave as one's mother. I resisted both roles, but in that refusal was often made to feel I was coming up short: Why not be friendly and light-hearted in rebuffing male students? Why make a big deal of it? (This was a suggestion made to me by a male colleague.) Why not be a shoulder to cry on for women students in trouble and who confessed their lives traumata? (This was a suggestion made to me by a female faculty member.)

I felt the unjust gendered weight of these student-professor interactions. It was clear this small subset of students, who saw me as a woman foremost and not so much as their professor, were acting on blatant gender bias that, because of their status as students, was difficult to unmask. When I brought up behavior I thought inappropriate to some of my supervisors over the years, several of them suggested that my attitude was the problem, not the inappropriate boundary-crossing behavior of the student. "Just be a nice (white) woman," was the underlying message.

One benevolent consequence of the inappropriate behavior of a small subset of my students is that I began to really enjoy and look forward to students of diverse backgrounds in the classes I taught: Because boundary-transgressing behavior of students almost always came from students who were white. This pattern was both painful to me and also eye-opening, making me understand better how structures of power, interlocking through codes of race and gender, give permission to some people to transgress others' boundaries. The structures of racial typographies being what they are, students of color oftentimes did not immediately see me as an oppressed class (woman), to whom they could unburden themselves, or onto whom they could project their erotic desires. But even if this connection with students of color derived from some complicated power dynamics, I think it led to some fruitful moments in teaching — for me — and hopefully in learning for my students.

Some white students, male and female alike, expressed sexism toward me. In contrast, subtle effects of racism likely shaped non-white students' sense that they would be more cautious about transgressing boundaries with their professor. Apart from the obviously racialized problematic of the pattern I describe above, what I learned from this racialized difference is that real teaching happens only when you are able to be a professor, not a woman, in your students' eyes.

As noted, most of the students at this university were white. However, in the Feminist Theory class that I will discuss now, for the final parable of this essay, the class was not majority white. The class appeared under the rubric of Sociology, and the Sociology major, at the university where I teach. To its credit, the Sociology major is one of the most racially diverse in student population. The enrollment for the specific class I am now discussing was extraordinarily cosmopolitan, with students from Greece, Ethiopia, Nigeria, and the Caribbean as well as students who were African American, Asian American, Native American, and white.

Before I knew the student composition of the class, I had already written the syllabus for that fall course. That summer I was, to be fair, bored by the thought of teaching feminist theory yet again. As non-tenure track faculty, I did not have the power within the university to voice my desire to teach a different course. So, since I had taught the class so many times before, I asked myself: What do I really care about in the field of feminist thought? I wanted to study theorists and schools of theory that were usually placed as glimpses in mainstream feminist theory courses. Rather than teaching predominantly white feminist theory (Judith Butler, *et. al.* and *ad nauseum*), with just a couple readings and lessons focusing on black feminist theory and/or Asian or Latina theorists, which is a typical Feminist Theory syllabus, instead I chose two books—not textbooks—to be the centerpieces of our semester's study: bell hooks's *Feminist Theory: Margin to Center*, and Mel Y. Chen's *Animacies: Biopolitics, Racial Mattering, and Queer Affect*.[5]

We read these two books in their entirety over the course of the semester, really getting inside the important work that hooks and Chen were leveraging. We also, later in the semester, did read some white theorists' essays. But I chose these two books mentioned above as the focus because hooks and Chen were theorists whose work I knew but did not know well and yet every time I read a quote, or short piece, by hooks or Chen I always thought, *Yes, I completely agree with that insight.* I wanted to know more about them. I was excited to center the class on these two excellent books by African American and Asian American feminists. I was not trying to represent race in the classroom. I was trying to keep myself interested and engaged in the books I was teaching, and I was trying to get to the heart of feminist theory. Why do we have feminist theory? bell hooks and Mel Y. Chen give real meaning to this theory.

A small number of white, women students in the class, however, believed they already knew what feminist theory was and believed I was not teaching it. By eschewing, just for one semester, the well-trodden path of white, wealthy, enshrined-by-the-academy feminists, I was upsetting a small number of white women students' sense of entitlement and ownership of feminism. Those two students' anger grew as the semester progressed. They complained that bell hooks was an aggressive writer, a harsh and unkind person. I did not budge: we were getting through that book! It was on the syllabus to stay. I thought, and think, that *Feminist Theory: from Margins to Center,* is a great book.

In their minds, however, the students began to fuse me with bell hooks, and hated me because — as an apparently white woman — they had expected something different from me.

This small group of white women, it seems, had expected that I would put them at the center of the class, not the non-white people who made up a significant part of the class. As white women of a certain income bracket, they felt sufficiently entitled, by dint of their race, to complain about my "harsh tone" in the classroom. This scene also becomes a parable: a parable of how race and gender intertwine with the power structures of the University.

I understand that the ostensible complaint was that I did not allow discussion of the rape of white women to be part of that particular semester's class.[6] But I'm equally certain that this situation did arise because I veered from the acceptable racial script that often calls for white women to teach white feminist theory, at least in a class that is titled Feminist Theory. To be clear, I was teaching in a class that was not by its title identified as intended to teach the work of non-white scholars. I taught a syllabus almost completely without using the majority work of white scholars. By veering from the script of race, I did not back down and thus my actions were interpreted as "harsh." Lastly, I had also veered from the script of gender, in that I had made clear that I did not want to act as mother to my students, but instead wanted to be their teacher, showing them how to think for themselves and re-think responsibilities and actions. For me, bell hooks and Mel Y. Chen wrote ideal texts for that endeavor.

Since that semester, I have been more careful, sad to say. Today, I still teach texts and materials that are written by, created by, and reflect histories and perspectives other than Eurocentrism. Nonetheless, I have reverted to the more expected script of having most of the material in classes that are not by their titles indicated to be about race be classes in which a predominance of material taught is written by or created by scholars of European origin. The theory of radical indigenous studies—in which indigenous perspectives are not taught as "samplers" on a table mostly filled with Euro-scholars, but instead are taught as *the* perspective is ultimately one that needs to be circulated and adopted in the university; not just within specialized courses, but also outside of it. This is the key truth that I learned from my traumatic experience teaching Feminist Theory: for a very small but vocal number of white women, being white means being the center.

For me, a white woman, to teach a class that did not give the perspective of whiteness the center was upsetting to them. If I had been teaching a course that was under the rubric of African American studies, I believe it would have been fine to teach bell hooks. But to teach a course that was titled simply Feminist Theory, well, it was upsetting for some white feminist students to take that class and be taught African and Asian American feminisms first and foremost, and at the center. Certainly, white perspectives matter and need to be taught, but they need to be taught as white perspectives, not as the global holistic truth. They need to be historicized. In my prose poem "Mary Wollstonecraft Died for My Sins," I try to atone for leaving out the work of early British feminist Mary Wollstonecraft that semester: Wollstonecraft is a great thinker, a great feminist.[7] Yes, teach white feminist writers, of course, but that needs to be just one part of teaching all feminisms; that is what feminism is about. I feel certain that were she alive today Mary Wollstonecraft, brilliant and original, would agree.

I no longer teach a course called Feminist Theory. I have retreated, for reasons of personal survival, from teaching any course that specifically and wholly contends with gender and feminism (even as these topics often inflect my teaching of other subjects). But I dream of being able to teach exactly such a course — called Feminist Theory—that makes race and race theory its heart. Because feminist theory has to be about power dynamics, it has to center on race. Such a class does not, in its title, indicate that it will deal with race, but fulfills a great need by dealing with it. As non-tenured faculty and without a stable contract, it would be a risk I am unable to take on anytime soon.

As the intertwining threads of this parable reveal, gender and race, once pulled in different directions, can easily get caught in a nexus of unvoiced and unspoken grief and what the social theorist Pierre Bourdieu aptly called "soft violence"—violence that is not physical but stems from social pressure and social punishment. A male professor would almost certainly not have faced the situation described above. Or, a female professor whose behavior fit gendered expectations (that is, who presented herself as motherly). I tell the parable not to indict specific actors (we are all human and we do the best we can moment to moment), but instead to point out and make clear that whiteness is preserved as a privileged rhetoric and a rhetoric of privilege, a claiming of center stage and central ground, even in the minds of young, apparently liberal, white women students. I learned from these students the most important lesson that I could have learned, as a teacher.

Feminism may not be enough to destabilize this unspoken place of entitlement in liberal studies and the humanities. Only the combination of critical race theory with feminist theory will be able to turn the tide for deeper thinking and societal change. This book is called the *Substance of Fire* because of the material consequences of gender and race, the way that we can say we are all equal but inequality emerges at the level of materiality: unequal access to power, unequal access to voice, and unequal access ultimately to cultural and "real" capital. The fire of gender and race runs mostly beneath the surface of the twenty-first century four-year university, which calls itself a place of equality. Gender and race are the substance of fire, often suppressed from the dialogue that overtly claims equality has been already achieved, but always beneath the surface, breaking out at points of tension.

End Note

I wrote this essay in June of 2017, before Charlottesville, Virginia, the city where I teach, became a national and even international symbol of violence and racism. For me, the events of August 11 and August 12, 2017, among many other responses (principal among them, the emotions of grief and fear), raised the question of what was it that made the "substance of fire," which is racism in America, leap forward at this time and place? What shifted so that racism expressed itself so openly, garishly, even murderously? And why here, in Charlottesville, which is a demographically left-leaning town, overall?

In some of the prose poems that follow, I meditate on these questions. In the prose writings of Riley Blanks and Blakeley Calhoun, alumna of the University of Virginia, the events of August 11 and 12, 2017, in Charlottesville, are thought-through. But, in the end, one is always at a loss for words in the face of violence. Our words approach the events, in hindsight, in aftermath, seeking understanding. ∎

WORKS CITED

1. Anthony Kwame Appiah, *The Ethics of Identity* (Princeton: Princeton University Press, 2007).

2. I have taught for various programs and departments over the course of the past eleven years. For me, it is important here to make clear that the class described in this essay was *not* an Art History class, the program for which I now teach.

3. Of course, feminist theory includes more than one strand. I refer the reader to the Combahee River Collective's statement, and also to the inimitable work of Teresa De Lauretis. These writers and workers in the field of feminism establish the kind of nuanced and deeply though approach that is truly feminist. See, Keeanga-Yamahatta Taylor *How We Get Free: Black Feminism and the Combahee River Collective* (Haymarket, 2017); see also, Teresa De Lauretis, *Figures of Resistance: Essays in Feminist Theory* (University of Illinois Press, 2007).

4. Roland Barthes, *Roland Barthes by Roland Barthes* Trans. Richard Howard (New York: Hill and Wang, 2010).

5. bell hooks *Feminist Theory: From Margin to Center* (New York: Routledge 2014); Mel Y. Chen *Animacies: Biopolitics, Racial Mattering, and Queer Affect* (Durham: Duke University Press, 2012).

6. Ironically enough, previous to teaching this class, I taught several semesters of courses about gender-based violence, for which I prepared and steeled myself to discuss the subject of the rape of women. But for this one semester I did not wish to deal with the topic, as I had just finished an exhausting study, interviewing student-survivors.

7. Mary Wollstonecraft, *A Vindication of the Rights of Woman* (Wollstonecraft Books, 2017)

"The poet…is there to articulate the necessity, but until the people themselves apprehend it, nothing can happen…Perhaps it can't be done without the poet, but it certainly can't be done without the people. The poet and the people get on generally very badly, and yet they need each other. The poet knows it sooner than the people do. The people usually know it after the poet is dead; but that's all right. The point is to get your work done, and your work is to change the world…When I say "poet" it's an arbitrary word."

—James Baldwin.
Conversations with James Baldwin (1989)
Eds. Fred Standley and Louis Pratt

SUBSTANCE OF FIRE:
POEMS & PROSE

FIRE

To walk away from a fire, turn toward it first,
recognize the story.
Sometimes a fire has to be put out.

But I walked away, and the fire kept burning,
pitting the scorch-
tasting, luminous earth.

Fire is sky bent inward.
I walked away, flat my soul.
But I had to save what I could—

Fire eats all materials, transforms the wound.
Afterward, I could taste the smoke
in my hair, the curtains, the bed—
when we touched, the smoke was our hands.

Effigy words. But of course, fire stood there f
the light so fierce none could breathe it,
and ever singe the rain's curve.

MAP OF FIRE

the sky are gla
everything disappears.

SNOW STUDY

At last we t
the papers
also the n

THE SUBSTANCE OF FIRE

Fire has the quality of mirror, changing
by sky and who or what stands before it.
Fire is not meant for shelter

sweep away

penances.

burning

after st

ne home

CHRISTIAN GIRL

In Sunday school, teacher said: you don't look like a good Christian
girl.
Already, I'd memorized the scriptures.
Still leaves of persimmon at the windows, luminous,
traced with church crayons.

At twelv
smashing
in my rig
at know

RAIN DELAYS

119

THE SUBSTANCE OF FIRE

Fire has the quality of mirror, changing
by sky and who or what stands before it.
Fire is not meant for shelter
but ashes, recursive, sweep away

what sky will sift, light's penances.
In the backyard, my father is burning
leaves and sticks, haulm, left over after storm.
There must be another way to come home

but I know only this one, substance of fire,
transmuting material scar.
Where grass gets charred, leaving a mark,
my shadow curves there, veer

of shallow roots stripped by singe.
When I grow up and disappear
sky will turn into fire, the one jewel
not to give away, even

at night parties in men's houses,
backyards tasting of dirt and torn grass,
and he's burning the rest to the east.
The substance of fire swallows itself.

No matter. This is the center of the world,
the place to never return.
I am not looking for mercy, but something so much colder.
Live oak unlatch their folios, clean and bitter.

FIRE

To walk away from a fire, turn toward it first,
recognize the story.
Sometimes a fire has to be put out.

But I walked away, and the fire kept burning,
pitting the scorch-
tasting, luminous earth.

Fire is sky bent inward.
I walked away, flat my soul.
But I had to save what I could—

fire eats all materials, transforms the wound.
Afterward, I could taste the smoke
in my hair, the curtains, the bed—
when we touched, the smoke was our hands.

Effigy words. But of course, fire stood there first—
the light so fierce none could breathe it,
and ever singe the rain's curve.

COAT OF FIRE

The woodcutters at the side of the highway,
where the car broke down, hewed a vivid forest.
At the last, elegy
must be written in stone.

Put on shoes and coat
of fire, walk out straight
into the field behind the house,
sumac with its stillness of blood,

another daughter
who never made good.

MAP OF FIRE

The bones of the sky are glass
that's why everything disappears.

Through laurel and live oak, vanish kestrel and kingfisher.
Through mirrors, my face and my sisters' go away.

I tried to save a map of the heavens
reflecting the apartments from which we'd been cast out.

One spring, charted the flickering of leaves—
new bones of the dogwoods, transpicuous cast,

done with apartments, rented a house,
stayed there even though the owner

threatened return, carrying his knife—
the knife of light writes what it writes.

Into sky everything goes away
diamond body of subsidence.

The bones of sky are ash, aftermath.

I listen for my mother's voice
because light has no root
but fire. So I wrote down this map to steady myself—

vermilion, maroon, burgundy fire of dusk.
In the kitchen mother burns supper
because she will not look.

RAIN DELAYS

The measure of stars is not distance but light,
and within light, fire's scintillance—

we keep asking what is the address,
where the flare should settle, fugitive

mirror, who will be
the one you save?

BIRD TRANSFORMATION
(after the Ana Mendieta work of this name)

It hurt when the feathers began to appear:
small dulse pulse, prick of blood,
as each stamen emerged,
fletchers, stuttered substance of flight—

transfiguration like and unlike the arrows of Sebastian—
my wounds came from the inside and worked out,
the way fire emerges through sky's skin.

Tentatively, I tried to set myself aloft
but feathers like fire catch the air uncontrollably.
To ease my flight, I starved, eating nothing but two apples per day,
until my bones grew hollow.

My clothes fit strangely, and women looked the other way.
Men were interested though, they watched the dark tumblers of my eyes—

what chance might catch, feathers opening
a thousand aleatory slant and slender bridges
between heaven and psalm. Was it terrifying?

Only in the way of eclipse, the island sinking

in gray dreams that have awakened me since childhood.
Shore birds cross and pass, above the city, cusp of rain at windows' eyelids.

The apartment buildings in this city of strangers rise
window by window, a fractured

gridded sky of pale stares.

The substance of feathers is odd, between bone and vein, sky and mirror,
between pelt, pelage, fur and skin, nothing
but air caught on narrow ridges,

a holographic drawing—
oaks flutter, a symptom of autumn.
Leaves unlatch to fly.

RETRACE

(after Hannah Arendt)

Retrace your steps, through the garden hard with rain, wet reflection
almost a painting: retrace your steps
through the body of rain without house,
other-worldly glistening,
your nerves on the order of rain, raw and open.

Retrace your steps, this time do not fall, do not turn
too quickly, losing balance, reflecting double from wet gravel.
Retrace your steps, understand they cannot be healed—
the old wounds—the same house and hour,
what has fallen has fallen, photographs

only vanish into the shelter of language.
Retrace your steps—walk back, out of rain's open star,
this time do not accept her hand
but cross alone, as far as you have to go.

ARS POETICA

At twelve, I fell
smashing the growth plates
in my right hand, the hand
that knows justice.

I had been turning
a back flip on the balance beam —
aerial fugitive, carrying in myself the emptiness
of sky, the way rain moves

above mom & pop stores
by the roadside, where they sell
gasoline, salt, apples, and tears — and I fell
out of time, dove down hard, hands first

to the cement floor, saved by my opened
right hand, that crushed like a spider.
Mother feared the hand
would never grow, after this accident,

that all my life I would keep the childish hand,
while the rest of my body opened
tall as a woman.
And it's true, I write even now

with the damaged hand, the side
that knows justice,
once broken,
the delicate web.

CHRISTIAN GIRL

In Sunday school, teacher said: you don't look like a good Christian girl.
Already, I'd memorized the scriptures.
Stiff leaves of persimmon at the windows, luminous,
uneasily traced with church crayons.

In Sunday school, I more than held my own,
numbering the psalms. The persimmon
unnerved me, though—red globes, and cranes overhead
opening sky— a whole sedge moves as one body.

The body of Christ transfigures to bread
scattered. A girl can be an unkind thing,
less than what's hoped for.
What does a good Christian girl look like?
Blonde hair, blue eyes, rosebud mouth.

Evening cranes disappear beyond
stripped trees in winter,
a formal shoal.

PRINCIPIA MATHEMATICA

As a child I loved numbers, they were my friends,
each number had a personality and in combination
the numbers became something mystical, even now
I keep secret the codes I found, just listening
to the sequences of the world inside — to tell them
would be like opening my chest, handing you my heart.

And so, in college, lone Ivy League girl
from the deep South, I chose to major in math,
and sat in the small autumn classroom
before the chair of the department, my hands shaking.
He looked straight at me: *"No one with that face
will ever be a mathematician."* Everyone in the room laughed.
It was not a compliment. I was the only girl.
Befitting my background, I wore an horizon of eye-shadow

azure blue, edging to purple. Next semester, switched majors
to philosophy, attending seminars with my girlfriend,
in her go-go boots and miniskirts,
a lightning rod I stood behind.
Philosopher: begin again, try
any language to mend this broken
material, almost
infinite world.

RED SWEATER

The last winter it was cold here, never a real winter afterwards, I wore
a red sweater, always, when walking into the University to teach,
then stripped down to a tee-shirt, so intense the indoor heating.
The first part of myself that I lost was that red sweater.
As soon as I got home I realized it was gone,
telephoned security, and the guard searched the entire building, room by room,
as I described to him again and again the color of the wool:
deepest red, not burgundy, not the color of blood nor poinsettias.
The color, maybe, of an apple on a cold day when the tree
stands almost emptied because it is already winter.
Described to him the weft of the cloth, the garment's size, extra
small, as I had been in hospital
with pneumonia the spring before, and lost twenty pounds. Nothing.
The night drew colder, an open door.
Next morning as I searched each classroom chair, only the ghosts
of my own words, an old lecture. So I think of it, sometimes, red sweater
I traded for a job, and how I loved the feel of that cloth,
not too soft, nor too heavy, but sufficient
for the purposes of true winter,
which has not returned since then, the last winter I wore
my heart on my sleeve, Corazon, Corazon,
gather me now, skin and bones.

SNOW STUDY

At last we threw everything out of the house:
the papers of his youth, master's thesis, dissertation work,
also the notes for every unwritten book.
We threw out his robes, bachelor's and doctoral.
There was no room left, the floorboards sinking down
like branches under heavy snow.

In the yard a few cardinals pecked then flew on;
nothing edible from the decades of language.
A radio played from a neighboring house
forecasting more snow.
So his belongings got covered with such transient ash,
tarnish while we waited a week for the Goodwill truck
to take away these apatite garments.

The papers had weighted the highest room in the house,
curled dog-eared by a statue of Ganesh in contraband ivory
from a century and artist's hand unidentified,
purchased on Portobello Road fifty years back; among the paper stacks
a few stray postcards from Alabama, and the Alhambra.
We laid into the yard his shoes and umbrellas.

It had to be done, had to be over.
Snow covered the childhood mirrors.

By evening, stripped trees came through
the skin of snow, stilling, stilling
the dark, real bones. Now the house will stand empty

and we'll begin again
with blank paper, to transpose
a language of necessity, curved and red and new.
Anagrammatic—for insects still move through
the gaps of winter, studying its hiemal heart,
every word a pulse.

BUYING FAST FOOD NEAR THE BORDER, CIRCA 1995[*]

We'd been driving through Louisiana forever, a decade
before the floods. In dry Texas at last
stopped for coffee and food.

Restaurant walls lined with photographic reproductions
of the executions of Mexican "bandits"—so read the captions
to oversized, shellacked images

celebrating the deaths of men who resisted
America's Texas. Nothing in the restaurant
told their actual histories, or names.

Just captions stating they were criminals caught by federales,
and citizen mobs, delivered to justice.
I never ate meat in those days, French fries

and coffee, salt and caffeine. Counting out fries,
stared at the cheap prints,
the faces of the condemned turned away,

swaying bodies blurred
in the camera's impassive exposure.
It's easy to get lost in America,

we were traveling with his R& B band,
a cheap apartment awaiting us in Austin.
The unseen eyes of the condemned

haunted me—they haunt me still, all that is
not shown but seen,
the bad dreams of hunted men.

Photographs stand
a kind of burned remnant, light's stain, the tracing of fire,
of who once breathed

on the earth. Easy to get lost
in America. The Colorado dries out, bending west,
its deep eddy sinks behind the apartment complex, sinks

deep as the eyes of hunted men
who found no sanctuary
in the borderlands.

---

*   For the history intimated by this poem, please see Richard Delgado, The Law
of the Noose: A History of Latino Lynching, 44 Harvard C.R.-C.L. L. Rev. 297
(2009).

Note: The first poem of this prose series is on the topic of lynching postcards, which were common in the American southeast between the late nineteenth- and early twentieth- century. The reader who wishes to learn more should consult the book Without Sanctuary by James Allen, John Lewis, Hilton Als and Leon F. Litwack. The specific background of my prose poem is an undergraduate course I taught from 2011 until 2015, at the University of Virginia, called "Violence in the Media." The course was an upper level seminar, geared to senior (fourth year) students. It was a small, seminar size class, and emphasized class discussion and research. We studied violence in movies, photography, and video games, through the lens of critical theory and cultural trauma theory. Each semester I taught a different syllabus—there is so much violence in the media, the materials I could have taught for this course were endless—and, as the poem notes, for three different semesters, the course included a section on lynching postcards. The students who took the class were a diverse group, but usually African American students were well represented in the class. These students seemed to relish the chance to talk—really talk—about lynching postcards and their legacy. I never showed these images in class, but referred the students to a now defunct website called withoutsanctuary.org that at the time showed the images on-line. My theory was that the trauma of looking at the images was such that each of us—myself included—should be in a position to control our manner, time, and quantity of such viewing. Hence, we would look at the photographs separately, but discuss them together. Two of the students, football players for the college, mentioned stories passed down to them by their grandmothers in regards to the history of lynching in the South. Those stories have weighed on my heart. ∎

TEACHING ABOUT LYNCHING PHOTOGRAPHS
IN CHARLOTTESVILLE, VIRGINIA, CIRCA 2010-2014

CLAIRE MILLIKIN

NOT A WHOLE SEMESTER, just one section of one University course I taught three times. We looked at images online, in private, each alone, discussed them in seminar, late afternoons for three autumns in Virginia, which is not where I'm from. Late afternoon light, sifting through stripped dogwood, shadowed the university walls. Two students said their grandmothers had told them how it used to be, how black folks were forced to come afterwards, see the corpse, learn the warning. Never allowed Christian burial by loved ones. Why did I decide to teach about these postcards, postcards I'd never seen except in books of scholars?

The names of the towns were also my lexicon of home, counties in Georgia being most numerous among the images of the dead, and all my dead buried in Georgia. Muscogee, Oxford, Newton, Cherokee. I recognized the forest from my childhood: longleaf pine, stripped red in autumn, shadowed in those photographs the hands of the dead. In the twenty-first century, we could look at lynching postcards online, *Without Sanctuary,* innocently, bear witness, I thought. But those kids, what their grandmothers had told them. Baby-faced students with broad

"As if we were holy in that place."

shoulders, who said they played football for Virginia to help their mothers. Tift County, also Savannah, low and deep the psalm of Christian burial denied the men whose ghosts held in lynching postcards. A three-week section of a course I taught three times, in Virginia, where I'm not from. But close enough. Cherokee County, Muscogee County, in Georgia, my ancestors buried there in quiet stain. A thousand hits a day, those college kids sustained, for their mothers, for Virginia.

The Survivors, circa 2007-2017

The student with blonde hair always came late to my class, or she'd not show up at all. Days would pass, we'd forget her, then she'd return, sitting stiff, as if cornered. But after class she'd linger, staring as I gathered my papers, eyes wide, mouth shut, and we'd walk together to the corner. The student with black hair stopped coming to my lectures, three weeks into the semester, but showed up for my office hours, every Friday morning at nine a.m., bringing two coffees, asking what she'd missed. I told her, every word, chapter and verse, giving the lectures charismatic shimmer, as if we were holy in that place. The student with hoop earrings wore sunglasses to seminar because—she told me—she was afraid to take them off and see the boys. The student who wore sweats and unbrushed hair showed up two weeks into the semester, sat at the table with hands folded, nun-like, on her closed notebook. When I asked her a question about the day's reading, she flinched. Later she wrote me an email, said she'd felt attacked. Someone sent me a follow-up note stating the student had been through an "unthinkable" event, left it at that, said it was *essential* that the student pass my class. Someone else told me about a gang rape. She never came back, all semester turned in no work. I gave her a C for the effort. She was a door of glass from which we looked away, to save our souls, to not see through to what she'd learned. And I am making here no straight confession: I am not speaking of anyone in particular, but of so many, called students at the university, but treated only like women there. Just get them through it, graduated, done, looking past the glass doors of their eyes.[1]

Mary Wollstonecraft Died for My Sins

A few students in that fall's Feminist Theory class—twenty-year-old white women with beautiful clothes, co-eds at a prestigious university—made a complaint. I was teaching Feminist Theory, but not the right kind. I was a woman, but not the right kind. I did not want to talk about rape in the classroom; they asked why I did not want to talk about rape during my office hours. I have my reasons for not wanting to hear about rape. My reasons are personal. For me, the classroom and office hours are places to talk about ideas that we learn from reading the books on the syllabus. That semester, these happened to be books written by women who were not white.

Mary Wollstonecraft, to the best of my knowledge, was never raped. She was definitely white. She died in childbirth at age 38, at the end of the eighteenth-century. While still alive, she wrote "A Vindication of the Rights of Woman" published in 1792.[2] She argued that the only reason women appeared to be intellectually inferior to men was because women's education was either nonexistent or inadequate. She argued that once women were taught the same curriculum as men, educated on a par with men, women would be as smart as men. She wanted women to read and think.

Many professors would begin a Feminist Theory Syllabus with an excerpt from Wollstonecraft's "Vindication." But I did not. I began my

Feminist Theory syllabus with bell hooks's *Feminist Theory*.[3] We read the whole book, beginning to end. A few white women students complained bitterly: I was teaching Feminist Theory, but not the kind they wanted. I did not talk about the rape of white women. Instead, I talked about female poverty and environmental racism.

Mary Wollstonecraft, a white woman born in England in 1759, died of childbirth for the following reason: the physician used his bare, unwashed hands to pull afterbirth from her womb, introducing infection. As she was dying, her septic convulsions became so severe the bed jerked across the room, slamming against the wall. After her death, her countrymen said that God had justly punished her: for having attempted to live through her intellect—a man's domain—she was punished as only a woman could be punished, death by childbirth. No vindication, no vengeance.

But the question lingers on why these young white women wanted so badly to speak of other women's rapes—they themselves were not survivors—that they shut down the voices of everyone else in the classroom, all the other women in the class who were not white. All that mattered to these students were the bodies of white women. Most of the women in the classroom were women of color. Some of us also were survivors, keeping our silence for safety.

Mary Wollstonecraft was a white woman, but I believe she wanted everyone to have the right to fight against oppression. I think of her often. I think often of her argument, in "A Vindication of the Rights of Woman," about how education is the key to equality, how deep it goes. I never planned to be a woman. It's just the way I look to others; it's out of my hands.

Teaching at the University of Virginia After August 12, 2017

1. Who are they?

Who are the University of Virginia graduates who grew up to become white Nationalists, leaders of fascist and racist movements? I know their names but not their stories, that is, I don't know their stories at the University of Virginia, where I have taught for eleven years; which classes they took, how they absorbed the idea that it is rightful to hate other people, to claim a "European" unity. As James Baldwin points out, whiteness is a category created for the social and economic oppression of people who do not have pale skin and eyes.[4] I married into a family of Greek-Americans, some from Alexandria, Egypt, with dark olive skin, curly black hair, emigrants who in mid-twentieth century America ironed their hair, and shortened names like Calliope to Kate.

The boundaries of whiteness are bitterly enforced: I am often perceived by other whites as not looking Anglo, or, WASP; a person with pale skin, yes, but the features are off, cheekbones too sharp, mouth too large—in Sunday school I was told, *you don't look like a Christian girl.* The state of Virginia provided the Confederate army its lead general, an Episcopalian, who apparently looked like a Christian. On August 13, after the general's statue caused a woman's death, I started to think about those men, graduates of the University of Virginia and white supremacist leaders; wondered about their experiences at Jefferson's academical village; thought about fraternities and the old boys network the fraternities hold in place. From where did the white supremacists who emerged in the twenty-first century from the University of Virginia learn their lessons of hatred? Did the university, this same university where I have taught over a decade, paid minimum wage, fail to teach them not to hate? Fail to teach them that we are all equal?

2. How to Teach Afterwards

A classroom should be a space where we can be calm, and safe, and think about the world, whatever aspect of the world we are studying, and most importantly where everyone is welcomed to listen and to speak and analyze what we see. A classroom should not be a place where people are punished for coming from any given background; it should be a place where woman, man, trans, cis, gay, straight, black, white, Latino/Latina, Native American, are all safe to speak and learn, a place where every student is considered equally likely to excel. A classroom should be kept clean; flaking paint and wasps flying around make it harder to concentrate. There should be some natural light in a classroom. Maybe a tree nearby, or at least always a visible sky.

How do we teach after white supremacists have formed a small army and invaded the university grounds? How do we teach when the leaders of these fascists were graduates from said university? How do we teach when some in the university admonished students who protested the white supremacists? I try to follow the books that I love, allow my students to love them too: words of Barthes, and Foucault; and photographs by MacIndoe, and Weems, show my students how to love the world of ideas. This is the only world that will save them. How to teach when the world is on fire: tell them in this room we are breathing clean light.

A classroom should be a place where we set aside fighting and take up the desire to understand, a place to read carefully and to see the world through other people's eyes. That is the core task of a classroom: to become actual readers. Read the world. How to teach after those who cannot read the common humanity we all share have invaded the place where you teach: how to teach after the world has been burned, again, yet again.

3. Center of the Universe

After the KKK and their compatriots got kicked out of the town where I live, on August 13, 2017, a man who had graduated from the university where I teach, a guy who identified himself as a white rights activist, promised they'd be back: "We will make this provincial town the center of the universe." He meant it as a threat to the mayor, who is Jewish. I gave thought to what it might mean to become the center of this guy's universe.

All my life I've been afraid of the center of my universe: the place where the world is terribly real. I've hidden, afraid of Georgia, because everyone I'm related to going back centuries lived and died and is buried there, and if you know anything about America, you know the state of Georgia is a violent place. The center of the universe is irretrievable. It got lost in the great explosion that created the universe, a crater of time. But it pulls, its weight of bad dreams and desire: mortal, human, deciduous, flawed, pulled like the sound of a distant train. There is only the center, what harms you and what you love; fight to keep these poles separate, because if they come too close the stars collapse. The center of the universe is my father walking through every door I locked.

When the violent men who honor Hitler and the Confederacy return to this town, this university, making it the center of their universe, I won't be surprised. But the universe will expel them, in due time: the moral universe will kick them into outer darkness where it's worse than being homeless, or molested, where they will reap the stench of fire.

4. Human

For a long time, in my childhood, I wondered what gave people voices. It went so far, I wondered why animals could not speak.

I took paper and laid it on the earth. Set paint beside the paper in flat dishes, and goaded the family dog, named Cynthia, to walk through the paint and onto the paper. I was seven years old. I interpreted her footprints as symbols, signs, voice — Cynthia of the moon.

Every silence hides a language. In the southeastern United States, where I am from, thousands of indigenous languages vanished before colonization was done. A few hung on: Muskogean. Typonomy, I study still: the Chattahoochee where my grandmother was buried.

Every language hides a silence. In the core of white supremacy is a longing for something that every human being needs: they want to be heard, have a voice. They want a homeland. Most Americans are orphans, lost from their ancestors' homeland, their origin. And it's true, even the white supremacists have a reason to long for what they lack: a voice, a homeland. They too are human.

5. Professor, from Cotton Country

In a classroom, you must tell the truth, but some don't want to hear it; in a classroom you must listen, but many don't want to speak of it. Some students dislike reading, some mistrust language. Language is a thread pulled in a raveling cloth. Time to change your garments. Traveling in the rusted red car, back down into Georgia every childhood spring, in and out open windows moths flew, carrying the souls of the dead. At night, riding by cotton fields I held onto nothing but moths and stars, floating through my hands in luminous distances. Back then, I could run faster than boys, breath for breath.

Cotton is violence: supplanting indigenous corn, Muscogee banished from their homeland, enslaved people forced to harvest. Speaking of cotton can never ease what happened in Georgia, where all my dead are buried. But language is a path, follow it at night back through the classroom where the sweater I lost still waits, red weft, frayed wrists, in a row of windows that turn night turns to mirrors. Put it on again, heart's garment, lost and found, teacher from cotton country, transla-tor of pain. ■

WORKS CITED

1. All characters described in this poem are composite, and in that sense fictional-ized, figures. Any resemblance to real persons is entirely accidental.

2. Mary Wollstonecraft, *A Vindication of the Rights of Woman* (Wollstonecraft Books, 2017)

3. bell hooks *Feminist Theory: From Margin to Center* (New York: Routledge 2014).

4. James Baldwin, *Collected Essays* (Library of America, 1998); See also, Patricia Hill Collins and Sirma Bilge *Intersectionality: Key Concepts* (Cambridge: Polity Press, 2016).

RICHARD
DELGADO

RICHARD DELGADO is a legal scholar and professor of law, currently at the University of Alabama. He is the author of several books and legal papers specializing in critical race theory, and is widely regarded as one of America's foremost critical race scholars.

N

OT LONG AGO, I was reflecting on higher education, the subject of this book. I had just published a law review article casting doubt on the possibility of reforming the system of corporate capitalism through law. I had concluded that Changes might be possible at the margins, as when Congress enacted the New Deal, but one should not count on more sweeping reform to arrive this way, for a thing cannot

transform itself and law and corporate capitalism are essentially the same thing. If one has limited time and energy (as most of us do), street activism, protest, and outright subversion are more promising avenues for achieving social change. A few new laws or stronger enforcement of existing ones may compel corporate actors to behave slightly better than they might otherwise, but they are unlikely to bring about broad social change.

What about educational reform? Popular as it is with liberals, I thought this avenue is just as unpromising as law for changing the economic system, and for much the same reason. Getting a college education may help a few from blue-collar families enjoy better lives than the ones they would have led if they had not gone to college, but we should not be under the illusion that this will go far to relieve economic inequality, much less lift the yoke of racial or sexual oppression under which many women and minorities labor at work or, as this book shows, at school. If this is correct, we should not be surprised that (a) campuses continue to be sites of racial and sexual oppression and (b) highly educated people, including minorities, are rarely at the forefront of social change.

I formerly held the hope that education potentially represents a subversive commodity reminiscent of the role labor plays in Marx's famous theory of surplus value. I reasoned that even a curriculum that starts out aiming to equip students with the bare knowledge to perform specific tasks (such as picking crops in the field) is likely to exceed its aims. If you set out to teach a young farmworker just enough to enable him or her to tend crops and spread the right amount of fertilizer at the right time of year, the worker is apt to read the warnings on the sack and sue you for poisoning their family. Education can easily end up inspiring a child to aspire to a better life than the one the adults have in mind for him.

I now realize that, unfortunately, the adults are likely to know this too and take steps to prevent it from happening. Moreover, such a learner may decide that cooperating with the adults is his best path to a middle-class life, such as crew chief. Consider the following examples showing that the abovementioned limitations are not merely hypothetical, but have actually materialized:

Curricular Reform in Tucson, Arizona:
Banned Books and Conservative Backlash
In Arizona, Latino immigrants have been under siege by private vigilantes who guard the state's Mexican border with shotguns and pickup

trucks, adding a further level of enforcement to a federal bureaucracy that they consider lacking in zeal. The former sheriff of Pima County (Joe Arpaio), many miles inland, devised a number of schemes to make life miserable for those suspected of illegal entry and ranchers living in the borderlands have added their efforts to his.

At about the same time, conservative legislators in the state capital passed a wide-ranging bill (SB 1070) that criminalized practically everything an unauthorized entrant might want to do including finding a job, renting an apartment, getting a ride from a friend, or sending his kids to school. Other states in the region and throughout the South followed suit.

A second measure sounded a cautionary note for the hope of reform through education. In Tucson, school authorities have been waging war against a popular Mexican American Studies (MAS) program in public schools with high enrollments of schoolchildren of Mexican descent. Established a few years earlier pursuant to a federal desegregation decree and taught by charismatic young teachers (some of them graduates of University of Arizona's ethnic studies department), the program had increased the graduation rate of Mexican American schoolchildren from barely fifty percent to nearly ninety.

The classes enabled students to learn about their own history, feel excited about school, and aspire to attend college, often the first ones in their families to do so. They learned about the great empires of Mesoamerica, the Mexican-American War, struggles for school desegregation, and Jim Crow laws under which black people had to sit in the balconies of movie theaters, take a back seat in restaurants, and swim in public pools only one day of the week, after which the pool would be drained and cleaned. They read novelists like Rodolfo Anaya, Sandra Cisneros, and critical theorists discussing America's sorry racial record. Many stayed up late at night devouring the books and discussing them with their parents and friends.

The authorities in the capital, however, did not like what they saw. Seeing the program as un-American, they enacted a second law (HB 2281) that forbade teaching ethnic solidarity and anti-American attitudes. Even though an outside audit gave the program a favorable review, the Tucson school board ended it anyway and, for good measure, banned certain texts that had found an eager readership of Latino teenagers. To make sure that everyone got the message, school employees boxed up the books in front of crying students and loaded them onto trucks bound for a warehouse outside of town. They also fired or transferred the young teachers who had filled the students with a keen appetite for learning. All this might remind readers of historical examples of book banning and carrying it out in front of the weeping schoolchildren as psychological torture. But the authorities explained their actions in quite different terms including age appropriateness, lack of curricular fit, and the need to reduce ethnic tension.

When the case (Arce v. Douglas) reaches the appellate level, judges will have to choose between two ways of looking at the abovementioned events. They could select a First Amendment prism, employing cases like Meyer v. Nebraska [(262 U.S. 390 (1923)] and Tinker v. Des Moines [(393 U.S. 503 (1969)], which upheld the First Amendment rights of students and parents vis-a-vis school authorities. Alternatively, they could emphasize a host of cases and statutes giving school authorities broad authority over curriculum and book selection.[1] This other line of cases gives the statewide discretion to determine what schoolchildren learn. And what the Arizona authorities want them to learn does not include material that can fill them with righteous indignation and a desire to change a system that oppressed their ancestors and dims their own chances. The appellate court is liberal; the Supreme Court is not. The ultimate disposition of the case is difficult to discern.

Liberal McCarthyism in the Seventies

The Tucson controversy concerns young students. What about the college-bound? With them, a natural experiment took place during the early 1970s when a large wave of black and Latino applicants, seventeen or eighteen years old, began knocking at the doors of America's colleges and universities in the wake of *Brown v. Board of Education* [347 U.S. 483 (1954)]. This cohort of undergraduates of color, who had entered the nation's newly desegregated schools a dozen or so years after the famous decision, their ranks swollen by affirmative action, promised to become the nation's first large generation of black and brown schoolteachers, social workers, mayors, university professors, lawyers, executives, and doctors.

Establishment figures were not at all eager for these future leaders to learn social analysis from left-wing professors of law, history, criminology, and political science, many of whom taught at elite schools like Harvard, Yale, and Berkeley. Having just lived through the turbulent sixties, academic visionaries such as Kingman Brewster, James Conant, Clark Kerr, and Albert Bowker hoped that the new cohort of minorities would turn out to be moderate, responsible, and above all

---

1. For example, *Island Trees School Dist. v. Pico,* 457 U.S. 853 (1982).

not angry. Accordingly, elite universities quietly removed white radical professors in a series of tenure denials that spread across the country during this period.[2]

A key qualification of an elite university president is the ability to spot a trend—to grasp large social currents, appreciate their relevance for the campus, and act accordingly. For example, will the next generation of students want to live in dorms or off campus? Will the adjunct faculty unionize and insist on better pay? Will alumni donations be up or down? Will molecular biology be the hot new field or will it be nanotechnology? Will minority enrollment continue to rise and will they primarily be African American, Latino, or Asian? What majors will they select? What will the Supreme Court decide about the future of affirmative action in the wake of *Fisher v. University of Texas* (2016)?

University presidents live or die by their ability to anticipate trends like these. By the early and mid-1970s, leading educational authorities could foresee the arrival of substantial numbers of post-*Brown* students of color beginning about a dozen years after that decision. What would they be like? Would they be as clamorous as the protesters who had roiled Berkeley, Michigan, and Yale just a few years earlier? Would they endorse violence and spout Mao, Marx, and Guevara as the black Panthers and Brown Berets had done only a few years earlier? Or would they be studious latter-day versions of Booker T. Washington leading their communities responsibly and peacefully into an era of harmony with whites?

---

2. Culling from newspaper reports and personal interviews, I showed how a number of these professors were forced out of their positions at elite universities and remade their careers at lower-level universities or changed their line of work entirely.

154

The speeches, personal writings, oral interviews, and memoirs of four prominent university leaders show that these questions were very much on their minds. They spoke about the shape and orientation of the new wave of minority students and hoped they would integrate peacefully into the campus scene, devote themselves to their studies, mix with white students, and move into leadership positions while serving as role models for the next generation of students of color. And they were especially wary of the role that white radical professors might play in socializing them.

This is not to say that each of these towering figures consciously aimed to rid their campuses of leftist professors to avoid corrupting minority youth, much less that they conspired with each other in a smoke-filled room. Much of their participation was indirect, but they set an example and tone and communicated, directly or indirectly, to their underlings the kind of campus they wanted, leaving it to the department heads, deans, and chancellors who ran the campus on a day-to-day basis to act accordingly. And the kind of campus they wanted was peaceful, with students of all types working together to create the kind of society that high-level technocrats prefer, with everything operating smoothly like a well-oiled machine.

Hard-core Marxists have written that race divides the working class. Whether that is true or not, a generation of promising left-wing professors lost their jobs at elite institutions in order that America's campuses might buy a short-lived racial peace.[3] They will see how, even at the

---

3. Interested readers may examine the full story of this era, see Richard Delgado, "Liberal McCarthyism and the Origins of Critical Race Theory," 94 *IOWA L. REV.* 1505 (2009). https://digitalcommons.law.seattleu.edu/faculty/153, Accessesd May 1, 2018.

college level, leaders keep a close watch on who is delivering instruction and to whom. When the combination of teacher, content, and learner promises a combustible mix, the establishment intervenes. The purge of the early 1970s (which swept Canada as well) is but one example of this mechanism in action.

Legal Education: When the Stakes Rise

When the students are old enough to attend law school, the stakes are even higher. Lawyers wield real influence; their actions shape what happens in the worlds of business, corporate finance, investment, banking, government, and criminal enforcement. Here, power replicates itself even more surely than it does when the students are younger. Consider two examples (the reader could no doubt think of many more):

1. Citations and What They Tell About the Shape of Legal Knowledge
Years ago, a young legal scholar noticed a curious feature of civil rights scholarship in the nation's top law reviews. The leading writers (all of them white, male, and liberal) cited mainly each other, ignoring the small but growing cohort of black and Latino scholars who were beginning to write in this arena. The author pointed out that this practice had real consequences, including distortions in the shape of legal knowledge. He described an informal sociogram showing who cited whom and noted that no matter where one entered this universe, one came to the same result: an inner circle of about a dozen white male writers who commented on, took polite issue with, and expanded on each other's ideas.

The failure to acknowledge minority scholarship extended even to non-legal propositions and assertions of fact such as the psychological harm of racism. He posited reasons why one might look with concern on a situation in which the scholarship about one group is written by members of another and how the prominent scholars, all of whom staunch liberals, could have unwittingly perpetrated this form of exclusion. He replicated the study ten years later, showing that a younger generation of legal scholars was following much the same practice as their elders.

Legal scholarship is, of course, only one part of what goes on in the legal academy. Teaching is another. Consider how informal controls on the nature and content of instruction shape the distribution of social power and influence.

2. Ideology and the Legal Classroom.
I recently had occasion to consider the role of legal education in major land-reform cases in two continents, three countries, and two American states. In *Mabo v. Queensland* [(No. 2) (HCA 1992)] 1992 WL 1290806], the Australian High Court overruled the longstanding doctrine of *terra nullius,* under which Australia had justified occupation of the entire subcontinent, which until then had been home to the Aborigines alone. Around this same time in Canada, *Calder v. British Columbia* [(AG) [1973] S.C.R. 313, [1973] 4 W.W.R. 1] reversed a similar legal tradition in that country.

As a result, national commissions are now returning large stretches of land in the two nations to native people. In the United States, persistent questions prompted Congress and the Government Accountability Office (GAO) to consider whether large tracts of government land in the Southwest had been improperly taken from Mexican people in the wake of the Mexican-American War and the Treaty of Guadalupe Hidalgo. One of five options the GAO offered for Congress's consideration was to return improperly seized land, now transformed by the government into national parks and forests.

In Colorado, the state Supreme Court in *Lobato v. Taylor* [71 P.3d 938 (Colo. 2002)] upheld an ancient land grant by a wealthy settler, Carlos Beaubien, that provided for the communal use of his property by Mexican villagers and their descendants for the purpose of hunting, fishing, and gathering firewood and water. The grant, which dated back to the time of the war with Mexico, turned on Mexican land-use practices that encouraged collective ownership and use. When in 1960 a lumberman from North Carolina purchased the Taylor Ranch and later began closing it off to nearby villagers, the Colorado court system was required to determine the legal effect due the original Beaubien document. When it did, it affirmed an early form of native possession and land use in the face of advancing free-market interests and values.

Remarkably, lawyers played very little role in all these landmark decisions. In *Mabo,* the driving force was Eddie Mabo, an indigenous gardener who enlisted the aid of a friendly history professor who began researching the origins of the doctrine of *terra nullius.* It was only after the historian, Henry Reynolds, wrote a book, *Law of the Land* (1987), and convened a student conference on land rights in Australia that lawyers entered in. In *Calder,* the driving force was a council of elders who began petitioning the Canadian government nearly a century earlier. Likewise in a New Mexico land revolt that presaged the events in Colorado, Lopez Reies Tijerina, an itinerant preacher with very little formal education, researched land titles in the county law library and, in Mexico City, began raising the question of who owned Kit Carson National Forest. And in *Lobato,* the attorneys of record were pro bono lawyers with Jewish-sounding surnames, not Latino-sounding ones.

Why so few lawyers in these landmark cases, especially ones of indigenous or minority background? By the time they arose, American law schools had been graduating Indian and Mexican American lawyers for several years. Yet not one seems to have played a major part in either of the American cases nor did Australian or Canadian lawyers play significant roles in initiating *Mabo* or *Calder*. Minority lawyers during this period were busy writing wills, filing divorces, and defending clients in criminal cases. But few took part in cases that changed land rights in their countries.

Why not? Perhaps young Latino or native Alaskan lawyers thought the cases too risky or insufficiently remunerative. They might have preferred that the land remain in Anglo hands since development—of the Taylor Ranch as a ski resort, for example—would have brought them more business than would returning it to small local farmers. But I believe the reason is simpler: We taught them white people's law and ways. We envisioned roles for them in much the same way university presidents did for the black and Latino undergraduates washing up on their shores in the early 1970s. We quietly cheered when one of them made partner or secured a position on an important state or federal commission. We did not teach them to use their legal skills imaginatively in the cause of sweeping social reform. We were pleased when most of them went on to careers indistinguishable from those of their classmates, wearing neat suits, speaking the same legalese, and advancing along conventional career paths.

Conclusion

If, as I have argued, corporate capitalism will not yield readily to legal reform, education is no magic talisman either. Examples ranging across three countries and several age groups show that the establishment prefers education that trains students for slots in the current system rather than as reformers transforming that system into a different one. Basic reform of entrenched patterns will only yield to outside pressure such as that accompanying a crisis or concerted popular mobilization. Self-education, critical writing, teaching, and scholarship can help instigate or inspire social change. But mass education supervised and overseen by watchful officials and beholden to a conservative citizenry in the thrall of moneyed interests is very unlikely to do so.

Social reform requires effort and will. One cannot delegate it to another profession (teachers or lawyers) or expect it to happen by enacting a few measures that spread the tax burden more equitably or boost wages slightly for those at the bottom. Those measures may be entirely commendable, but they will not transform an economic system that perpetuates inequality by its own weight. Nor will they turn the public education system (whether of the K-12, the undergraduate, or the professional variety) into an engine of change and transformation. That requires teachers and professors willing to depart from the prescribed text and take real chances with their careers. And it requires students and administrators willing to tolerate, support, and listen to them and others like the authors of this book.■

—Seattle, January 2018

OTHER BOOKS BY 2LEAF PRESS

2LEAF PRESS challenges the status quo by publishing alternative fiction, non-fiction, poetry and bilingual works by activists, academics, poets and authors dedicated to diversity and social justice with scholarship that is accessible to the general public. 2LEAF PRESS produces high quality and beautifully produced hardcover, paperback and ebook formats through our series: *2LP Explorations in Diversity, 2LP University Books, 2LP Classics, 2LP Translations, Nuyorican World Series,* and *2LP Current Affairs, Culture & Politics.* Below is a selection of 2LEAF PRESS' published titles.

2LP EXPLORATIONS IN DIVERSITY

Substance of Fire: Gender and Race in the College Classroom
by Claire Millikin
Foreword by R. Joseph Rodríguez, Afterword by Richard Delgado
Contributed material by Riley Blanks, Blake Calhoun and Rox Trujillo

Black Lives Have Always Mattered
A Collection of Essays, Poems, and Personal Narratives
Edited by Abiodun Oyewole

The Beiging of America:
Personal Narratives about Being Mixed Race in the 21st Century
Edited by Cathy J. Schlund-Vials, Sean Frederick Forbes and Tara Betts
with an Afterword by Heidi Durrow

What Does it Mean to be White in America?
Breaking the White Code of Silence, A Collection of Personal Narratives
Edited by Gabrielle David and Sean Frederick Forbes
Introduction by Debby Irving and Afterword by Tara Betts

2LP UNIVERSITY BOOKS
Designs of Blackness, Mappings in the Literature and Culture of African Americans
A. Robert Lee
20TH ANNIVERSARY EXPANDED EDITION

2LP CLASSICS
Adventures in Black and White
by Philippa Schuyler
Edited and with a critical introduction by Tara Betts

Monsters: Mary Shelley's Frankenstein and Mathilda
by Mary Shelley, edited by Claire Millikin Raymond

2LP TRANSLATIONS
Birds on the Kiswar Tree
by Odi Gonzales, Translated by Lynn Levin
Bilingual: English/Spanish

Incessant Beauty, A Bilingual Anthology
by Ana Rossetti, Edited and Translated by Carmela Ferradáns
Bilingual: English/Spanish

NUYORICAN WORLD SERIES
Our Nuyorican Thing, The Birth of a Self-Made Identity
by Samuel Carrion Diaz, with an Introduction by Urayoán Noel
Bilingual: English/Spanish

Hey Yo! Yo Soy!, 40 Years of Nuyorican Street Poetry,
The Collected Works of Jesús Papoleto Meléndez
Bilingual: English/Spanish

LITERARY NONFICTION
No Vacancy; Homeless Women in Paradise
by Michael Reid

The Beauty of Being, A Collection of Fables, Short Stories & Essays
by Abiodun Oyewole

164

WHEREABOUTS: Stepping Out of Place,
An Outside in Literary & Travel Magazine Anthology
Edited by Brandi Dawn Henderson

PLAYS
Rivers of Women, The Play
by Shirley Bradley LeFlore, with photographs by Michael J. Bracey

AUTOBIOGRAPHIES/MEMOIRS/BIOGRAPHIES
Trailblazers, Black Women Who Helped Make America Great
American Firsts/American Icons
by Gabrielle David

Mother of Orphans
The True and Curious Story of Irish Alice, A Colored Man's Widow
by Dedria Humphries Barker

Strength of Soul
by Naomi Raquel Enright

Dream of the Water Children:
Memory and Mourning in the Black Pacific
by Fredrick D. Kakinami Cloyd
Foreword by Velina Hasu Houston, Introduction by Gerald Horne
Edited by Karen Chau

The Fourth Moment: Journeys from the Known to the Unknown, A Memoir
by Carole J. Garrison, Introduction by Sarah Willis

POETRY
PAPOLíTICO, Poems of a Political Persuasion
by Jesús Papoleto Meléndez,
with an Introduction by Joel Kovel and DeeDee Halleck

Critics of Mystery Marvel, Collected Poems
by Youssef Alaoui, with an Introduction by Laila Halaby

shrimp
by jason vasser-elong, with an Introduction by Michael Castro

The Revlon Slough, New and Selected Poems
by Ray DiZazzo, with an Introduction by Claire Millikin

Written Eye: Visuals/Verse
by A. Robert Lee

A Country Without Borders: Poems and Stories of Kashmir
by Lalita Pandit Hogan, with an Introduction by Frederick Luis Aldama

Branches of the Tree of Life
The Collected Poems of Abiodun Oyewole 1969-2013
by Abiodun Oyewole, edited by Gabrielle David
with an Introduction by Betty J. Dopson

2Leaf Press is an imprint owned and operated by the Intercultural Alliance of Artists & Scholars, Inc. (IAAS), a NY-based nonprofit organization that publishes and promotes multicultural literature.

NEW YORK
www.2leafpress.org